President Heber C. Kimball's Journal

by

Heber C. Kimball

President Heber C. Kimball's Journal
by Heber C. Kimball

ISBN: 978-93-59326-07-8

Published by

DOUBLE 9 BOOKS

2/13-B, Ansari Road, Daryaganj
New Delhi – 110002
info@double9books.com
www.double9books.com
Tel. 011-40042856

ABOUT THE AUTHOR

"President Heber C. Kimball's Journal" is a historical document authored by President Heber C. Kimball himself. Heber C. Kimball was a member of the Quorum of the Twelve Apostles in The Church of Jesus Christ of Latter-day Saints (LDS Church) during the nineteenth century. The plot contains several surprising twists and turns that will keep the reader interested. Readers are compelled to continue reading because they want to know what happens next because the title character is so self-indulgent. Some stories are lethal and bizarre, while others creep up on you and slowly consume you. Kimball's notebooks offer unique insights into the early history, development, problems, and personal experiences of the LDS Church. Kimball discussed his missionary work, including trips to England where he assisted in the conversion of hundreds of people. President Heber C. Kimball's books include firsthand recollections of his interactions with other major early church leaders like as Joseph Smith, Brigham Young, and other Quorum of the Twelve Apostles members. Heber Chase Kimball was born on June 14, 1801 in Sheldon, Franklin County, Vermont. He was descended from the Kimballs, who arrived in Massachusetts from England in 1634. He was named after Judge Heber Chase, who assisted the family in settling in the area. His father, Solomon F. Kimball, was a blacksmith who also ran a farm.

CONTENTS

PREFACE

No apology is necessary for publishing as a volume of the "FAITH-PROMOTING SERIES" some portion of the history of the late President Heber C. Kimball. Knowing the estimation in which he was held while living by the Latter day Saints universally, and that the memory of his virtues and life-long devotion to the cause of God is still fresh in their hearts, we feel assured that they will regard as an acceptable offering the brief account of his experience contained in this volume. We only regret that we cannot in the present work give a sketch of his entire life, or at least all of those incidents from it which would tend to promote faith in young readers. His was an exceedingly active and interesting life, and it is scarcely necessary to state that the sketch here published, covering a period of only a little over four years, contains but a fraction of that which is interesting and wonderful in his life's experience. However, what is here given will doubtless convey many valuable lessons to those who read it, and will serve to indicate the character of the great man of whom it treats.

Heber Chase Kimball was one of the greatest men of this age. There was a certain nobility about his appearance as well as his disposition that would have made him conspicuous in any community, and the Church of Jesus Christ afforded ample scope for the exercise of his ability, and the trying scenes through which he passed called into play his best powers.

He was a man of commanding presence, with eyes so keen as to almost pierce one through, and before which the guilty involuntarily quailed. He was fearless and powerful in rebuking the wrong-doer, but kind, benevolent and fatherly to the deserving. He possessed such wonderful control over the passions of men, combined with such wisdom and diplomacy that the Prophet Joseph Smith called him "the peace-maker." His great faith, zeal, earnestness, devotion to principle, cheerfulness under the most trying circumstances, energy, perseverance and honest simplicity marked him as no ordinary man. He possessed great natural force and strong will power, yet in his submission to the Priesthood and obedience to the laws of God he set a pattern to the whole Church. His example throughout life was one of which his posterity may ever think with pride, and which the Saints generally will do well to follow.

No man, perhaps, Joseph Smith excepted, who has belonged to the Church in this generation, ever possessed the gift of prophecy to a greater degree than Brother Kimball. Although not at all pretentious, he was somewhat celebrated among his acquaintances for his prophetic inspiration. The prediction which he made soon after the arrival of the Pioneers in Salt Lake Valley, that the destitute Saints would soon be supplied with clothing, and that "States goods" would be sold in Salt Lake City as cheap as in New York, seemed most unreasonable at the time it was uttered. Its fulfillment, however, by the unexpected influx of gold-seekers, making their way to California, and anxious to lighten their loads by selling their goods at almost any price, is now a matter of history. Scores of other predictions were made by him and as literally fulfilled.

Brother Kimball was the only one of his father's family who embraced the gospel, but now his is one of the most numerous families in the Church. At the time of his death, which occurred June 22, 1868, he was the father of sixty-five children, of whom thirty males and eleven females were then living. His direct descendants now number one hundred and seventy-two.

The first ten chapters of this work were formerly published in pamphlet form by Elder R. B. Thompson in Nauvoo. Only a small edition, however, was printed, and it has now been out of print for a great many years. The next six chapters have been compiled from the manuscript history of Elder Kimball by his eldest daughter, Sister Helen Mar Whitney, to whom we are also indebted for the items contained in his letters from which the last chapter was written.

THE PUBLISHER.

CHAPTER I

The labors of the Elders of the Church of Latter-day Saints in early days were confined to the United States of America, with the exception of the province of Upper Canada, where a great many persons embraced the gospel of Jesus Christ, and rejoiced in the blessings thereof. The majority of this latter class were originally from Great Britain, and they soon began to manifest a desire that their relatives and friends who were still residing there, might be privileged with hearing the glad tidings of salvation, and be made partakers of those gifts and blessings which are promised in obedience thereto. For the attainment of this object, their prayers were continually ascending to the Lord of sabaoth, that He would prepare the way, and hasten the time when

> "The servants of the Lord
> Soon should take their stand,
> And spread the glorious light of truth —
> Throughout their native land."

Notwithstanding this desire, the way was not open for the Elders until the spring of 1837, when the word of the Lord to the Elders of Israel was, that they might go forth to the distant nations of the earth, that the kingdom might roll forth, so that every heart might be penetrated.

Prior to this, my labors had been confined to my own land, in which I had traveled about six thousand miles, preaching the gospel to the best of my ability, and had the pleasure of baptizing several of my countrymen for the remission of sins, and introducing them into the kingdom which the Lord has set up in these last days.

I had frequently felt a desire to visit the shores of Europe, and believed that the time was fast approaching when I should take leave of my own country and lift up my voice to other nations, warning them of the things which were coming on the earth, and making known to them the great things which the Lord had brought to pass. Yet it never occurred to my mind that I should be one of the first commissioned to preach the everlasting gospel on the shores of Europe, and I can assure my friends I was taken by surprise when I was informed by Brother Hyrum Smith, one of the Presidency of the Church, that I had been designed by the Spirit, and, at a conference of the authorities of the Church which had been held, was appointed to take the charge of a mission to the kingdom of Great Britain.

The idea of being appointed to such an important office and mission was almost more than I could bear up under. I felt my weakness and unworthiness, and was nearly ready to sink under the task which devolved upon me, and I could not help exclaiming: "O Lord I am a man of 'stammering tongue,' and altogether unfit for such a work. How can I go to preach in that land, which is so famed throughout Christendom for light, knowledge and piety, and as the nursery of religion; and to a people whose intelligence is proverbial?"

Again, the idea of leaving my family for so long a time, which a mission to that country must necessarily require — of being separated from my friends whom I loved, and with whom I had enjoyed many blessings and happy seasons — of leaving my native land to sojourn among strangers in a strange land, was almost overwhelming.

However, all these considerations did not deter me from the path of duty. Neither did I confer with flesh and blood; but the moment I understood the will of my Heavenly Father, I felt a determination to go at all hazards, believing that He would support me by His almighty power, and endow me with every qualification I needed.

Although my family were dear to me, and I should have to leave them almost destitute, I felt that the cause of truth, the gospel of Christ, outweighed every other consideration; and I felt willing to leave them, believing that their wants would be provided for by that God who taketh care of sparrows and who feedeth the young ravens when they cry.

I was then set apart, along with Elder Hyde, who was likewise appointed to that mission, by the laying on of the hands of the Presidency, who agreed that Elders Goodson, Russell, Richards, Fielding and Snider should accompany us.

After spending a few days in arranging my affairs and settling my business, on the thirteenth day of June, A. D. 1837, I bade adieu to my family and friends, and the town of Kirtland, where the house of the Lord stood, in which I had received my anointing, and had seen such wonderful displays of the power and glory of God. In company with Elder Hyde and the other brethren, I arrived at Fairport, on Lake Erie, that afternoon, a distance of twelve miles; and about an hour after our arrival, took passage in a steamboat for Buffalo, New York.

We were accompanied by Brother R. B. Thompson and wife, who were on their way to Canada, from Kirtland, where he intended to labor in the ministry.

After a pleasant voyage, we reached Buffalo the next day, at which place we expected to get some funds which were promised us, to assist us on our journey, but we were unfortunately disappointed.

At that time we had but very little means, but still we determined to prosecute our journey, believing that the Lord would open our way.

We accordingly continued our journey, and took our passage in a line boat on the Erie Canal to Utica, a distance of two hundred and fifty miles, and thence to Albany on the railroad.

From this latter place I went with Brother Richards into the country about thirty miles, where we were successful in obtaining some means to enable us to prosecute our journey. We then returned and took passage on a steamboat for New York, at which place we arrived on the 22nd day of June.

On our arrival we met with Brothers Goodson and Snider, according to appointment (they having gone round by the way of Canada), all in good health.

When we arrived at New York we found a vessel ready to sail, but not having sufficient means we were obliged to wait until such time as we could obtain funds to pay our passage and buy provisions for the voyage. We rented a small room in a store house, hoping that some way would be provided for us to go forward and fulfill the mission whereunto we were sent.

We spent considerable time while we were there in praying to our Heavenly Father for His guidance and protection, that He would make our way plain before us, bless us with a prosperous voyage across the billows of the mighty ocean, and make us a blessing to each other and to the captain and crew with whom we should sail.

During our stay in that city, we were subject to many inconveniences. We had to lay upon the floor, and had to buy and cook our own victuals; yet none of these things moved us, neither did we feel discouraged, believing that the Lord would open our way and guide us to our destination.

We conversed with many persons on the subject of the gospel, and distributed a large number of copies of the "Prophetic Warning" among all classes of the community; not forgetting the ministers of religion who abound in that city. We sent a copy to every one whose name we could ascertain through the medium of the post office.

After remaining a few days, we were presented with sixty dollars to assist us. Brother Elijah Fordham made us a present of ten dollars, and concluded to accompany us on our mission, but upon more mature consideration, we thought it was best for him to stop in that place, believing that the Lord had a people in that city, and that a Church would be built up, which was afterwards done by the instrumentality of Elders Parley P. and Orson Pratt.

Having obtained as much money as would pay our passage across the Atlantic, we laid in a stock of provisions, and on the first day of July went on board the ship *Garrick*, bound for Liverpool, and weighed anchor about ten o'clock, a. m., and about four o'clock, p. m. of the same day, lost sight of my native land. I had feelings which I cannot describe when I could no longer behold its shores, and when I bade adieu to the land of my birth, which was fast receding, I felt to exclaim:

> "Yes, my native land, I love thee:
> All thy scenes I love them well:
> Friends, connections, happy country,
> Can I bid you all farewell?
> Can I leave you
> Far in distant lands to dwell?"

However, when I reflected on the causes which had induced me to leave it for a while, and the work which devolved upon me I could likewise say,

> "I go, but not to plough the main
> To ease a restless mind."

No; I hope I was actuated by a different motive than either to please myself or to gain the riches and applause of the world; it was a higher consideration than these that induced me to leave my home. It was because a dispensation of the gospel had been committed to me, and I felt an ardent desire that my fellow-creatures in other lands, as well as those of the land of my birth, might hear the sound of the everlasting gospel, obey its requisitions, rejoice in the fullness and blessings thereof and escape the judgments which were threatened upon the ungodly.

Our passage was very agreeable, and the winds for most part very favorable. On the banks of Newfoundland we saw several whales and many different species of fish.

We were kindly treated while on board, both by the officers and crew, and their conduct was indeed praiseworthy; had we been their own relatives, they could not have behaved more kindly or have treated us better. Thus the Lord answered our prayers in this respect, for which I desire to praise His holy name.

The Lord also gave us favor in the eyes of the passengers, who treated us with the greatest respect. During our voyage a child belonging to one of the passengers was very sick and was given up for dead by the doctor who attended it; consequently, its parents had given up all hopes of its recovery, and expected to have to commit their little one to the ocean. Feeling a great anxiety for the child, I went to its parents and reasoned with, and laid before them the principle of faith, and told them that the Lord was able to restore their child, notwithstanding there was no earthly prospect of its recovery, to which they listened with great interest. Having an opportunity shortly after, secretly to lay hands upon the child, I did so, and in the name of Jesus Christ rebuked the disease which preyed upon its system. The Spirit of the Lord attended the administration, and from that time the child began to recover, and two or three days after it was running about perfectly well. Its parents had to acknowledge that it was healed by the power of the Almighty.

The last Sunday we were on the water I went to the captain and asked the privilege for one of us to preach on board. He very obligingly agreed, and appointed the time when it would be most suitable for himself and the crew to attend, which was at one o'clock p. m. We then appointed Brother Hyde to speak, and notified the crew and passengers of the circumstance.

At the time appointed, there was a congregation of from two to three hundred persons assembled on the deck, who listened with great attention and deep interest to the discourse, which was delivered with great power. I think I never heard Brother Hyde speak with such power and eloquence as that time; he spoke on the subject of the resurrection. The time being limited on account of the duties of the ship's company, his subject was necessarily condensed. The congregation was composed of persons from different nations, and of different faiths, English, Irish, Scotch, Germans, French, etc., both Jews and Christians. A great feeling was produced upon the minds of the assembly, who had never heard the subject treated in like manner before, and from the conversation we afterwards had with several of them, I believe that good was done and many from that time began to search the scriptures for themselves, which are able to make men wise unto salvation.

On the 15th of July we came in sight of land, which caused joy and gratitude to my Heavenly Father to arise in my bosom for the favorable passage we had had so far and the prospect of soon reaching our destination. We then sailed up the Irish channel, having Ireland on our left and Wales on our right. The scenery was very beautiful and imposing.

Three days after first seeing land, being the 18th of July, we arrived in Liverpool, one of the largest ports in Great Britain, being just seventeen days and two hours from our departure from New York. The packet ship *South America*, which left New York the same time we did, came in a few lengths behind. The sight was very grand to see these two vessels enter port, with every inch of canvass spread. When we first got sight of Liverpool, I went to the side of the vessel and poured out my soul in praise and thanksgiving to God for the prosperous voyage and for all the mercies which He had vouchsafed to me, and while thus engaged, and while contemplating the scenery which then presented itself and the circumstances which had brought me thus far, the Spirit of the Lord rested upon me in a powerful manner; my soul was filled with love and gratitude, and was humbled within me, while I covenanted to dedicate myself to God and to love and serve Him with all my heart.

Immediately after we anchored, a small boat came alongside, and several of the passengers, with Brothers Hyde, Richards, Goodson and myself got in and went on shore. When we were within six or seven feet from the pier, I leaped on shore, and for the first time in my life stood on British ground, among strangers whose manners and customs were different from my own. My feelings at that time were peculiar, particularly when I realized the object, importance and extent of my mission and the work to which I had been appointed and in which I was shortly to be engaged.

CHAPTER II

TIMIDITY AT THE THOUGHTS OF MY TASK—PROMPTED BY THE SPIRIT TO GO TO PRESTON—THE "TRUTH WILL PREVAIL"—MEET ELDER FIELDING'S BROTHER, A PREACHER—INVITED TO PREACH IN HIS CHAPEL—SEEING HIS CRAFT ENDANGERED, HE CLOSES HIS DOORS AGAINST US—ANOTHER MINISTER FORBIDS US BAPTIZING HIS CHURCH MEMBERS—DESPERATE STRUGGLE WITH EVIL SPIRITS—COMMENCE BAPTIZING—ELDERS SEPARATE—OPPOSED BY A MINISTER—HIS SUBSEQUENT SHAME.

The idea of standing forth and proclaiming the gospel in a land so much extolled for religion, which was constantly sending forth her ministers to almost every nation under heaven, and among a people who, of course, did not expect to be taught, but to teach others the principles of the gospel, and the consciousness of my own weakness and unfitness for such an undertaking, led me to cry mightily to the Lord for wisdom and for that comfort and support which I so much needed. At the same time I thought that if I could have been relieved from the responsibility which rested upon me, by fighting Goliath on as unequal terms as David did, I should have felt myself happy.

However, I endeavored to put my trust in God, believing that He would assist me in publishing the truth and that He would be a present help in the time of need.

Having no means, poor and penniless we wandered in the streets of that great city, where wealth and luxury, penury and want abound. I there met the rich attired in the most costly dresses, and the next moment was saluted with the cries of the poor, who were without covering sufficient to screen them from the weather. Such a distinction I never saw before. We then looked out for a place to lodge in, and found a room belonging to a widow which we engaged for a few days.

The time we were in Liverpool was spent in council and in calling on the Lord for direction, so that we might be led to places where we should be most useful in proclaiming the gospel and in establishing and spreading His kingdom. While thus engaged, the Spirit of the Lord, the mighty power of

God, was with us, and we felt greatly strengthened, and a determination to go forward, come life or death, honor or reproach, was manifested by us all. Our trust was in God, who we believed could make us as useful in bringing down the kingdom of Satan as He did the rams' horns, in bringing down the walls of Jericho and in gathering out a number of precious souls who were buried amidst the rubbish of tradition, and who had none to show them the way of truth.

Feeling led by the Spirit of the Lord to go to Preston, a large manufacturing town in Lancashire, we started for that place three days after our arrival in Liverpool. We went by coach and arrived on Saturday afternoon about four o'clock. After unloading our trunks, Brother Goodson went in search of a place of lodging, and Brother Fielding went to seek a brother of his, who was a minister, residing in that place.

It being the day on which their representatives were chosen, the streets presented a very busy scene; indeed I never witnessed anything like it before in my life.

On one of the flags, which was just enrolled before us the moment the coach reached its destination, was the following motto: "TRUTH WILL PREVAIL," which was painted in large, gilt letters. It being so very seasonable and the sentiment being so appropriate to us in our situation, we were involuntarily led to exclaim, "Amen! So let it be."

Brother Goodson having found a room where we could be accommodated, which belonged to a widow woman, situated in Wilford Street, we moved our baggage there. Shortly after, Brother. Fielding returned, having found his brother, who requested to have an interview with some of us that evening. Accordingly, Elders Hyde, Goodson and I went and were kindly received by him and Mr. Watson, his brother-in-law, who was present at the time.

We gave them a short account of the object of our mission and the great work which the Lord had commenced, and conversed upon those subjects until a late hour. The next morning we were presented with half a crown, which Mr. Fielding's sister had sent us.

It being Sunday, we went to hear Mr. Fielding preach. After he had finished his discourse, and without being requested by us, he gave out an appointment for some one of us to preach in the afternoon.

It being noised abroad that some Elders from America were in town and were going to preach in the afternoon, a large concourse of people assembled to hear us. It falling to my lot to speak, I called their attention to the first principles of the gospel, and told them something of the nature of the work which the Lord had commenced on the earth. Brother Hyde afterwards bore testimony to the same, which I believe was received by many with whom I afterwards conversed.

Another appointment was given out for us in the evening, at which time Brother Goodson preached and Brother Fielding bore testimony. An appointment was then made for us on Wednesday evening at the same place, at which time Elder Hyde preached. A number now being convinced of the truth, believed the testimony and began to praise God and rejoice exceedingly that the Lord had again visited His people, and sent His servants to lay before them the doctrine of the gospel "and the truth as it is in Jesus."

The Rev. Mr. Fielding, who had kindly invited us to preach in his chapel, knowing that quite a number of his members believed our testimony and that some were wishful to be baptized, shut his doors against us and would suffer us to preach no more in his chapel. For an excuse, he said that we had preached the doctrine of baptism for the remission of sins, contrary to our arrangement with him.

I need scarcely assure my friends that nothing was said to him from which any inference could be drawn that we should suppress the doctrine of baptism. No! We deemed it too important a doctrine to lay aside for any privilege we could receive from mortals. Mr. Fielding understood our doctrines even before we came there, having received several communications from his brother Joseph, who wrote to him from Canada, explaining the doctrines of the Church of Jesus Christ of Latter-day Saints. We likewise had conversed with him on the subject at our former interview. However, he having been traditioned to believe in infant baptism, and having preached and practiced the same a number of years, he saw the situation he would be placed in if he obeyed the gospel. Notwithstanding his talents and standing in society, he would have to come into the sheepfold by the door; and after all his preaching to others, have to be baptized himself for the remission of sins by those who were ordained to that power.

These considerations undoubtedly had their weight upon his mind, and caused him to act as he did, and notwithstanding his former kindness he soon became one of our most violent opposers.

An observation which escaped his lips shortly after this circumstance, I shall here mention. Speaking one day respecting the three first sermons which were preached in that place, he said that "Kimball bored the holes, Goodson drove the nails and Hyde clinched them."

However, his congregation did not follow his example; they had for some time been praying for our coming, and had been assured by Mr. Fielding that he could not place more confidence in an angel than he did in the statements of his brother respecting this people. Consequently, they were in a great measure prepared for the reception of the gospel, probably as much so as Cornelius was anciently.

Having now no public place to preach in, we began to preach in private houses, which were opened in every direction, while numbers believed the gospel. After we had been in that place eight days, we began to baptize in the name of the Lord Jesus for the remission of sins. One "reverend" gentleman came and forbid us baptizing any of his members; but we told him that all who were of age and requested baptism we should undoubtedly administer that ordinance to.

One Saturday evening I was appointed by the brethren to baptize a number the next morning in the river Ribble, which runs through that place. By this time, the adversary of souls began to rage, and he felt a determination to destroy us before we had fully established the gospel in that land; and the next morning I witnessed such a scene of satanic power and influence as I shall never forget while memory lasts.

About day-break, Brother Russell (who was appointed to preach in the market-place that day), who slept in the second story of the house in which we were entertained, came up to the room where Elder Hyde and I were sleeping and called upon us to arise and pray for him, for he was so afflicted with evil spirits that he could not live long unless he should obtain relief.

We immediately arose, laid hands upon him and prayed that the Lord would have mercy on His servant and rebuke the devil. While thus engaged, I was struck with great force by some invisible power and fell senseless on the floor as if I had been shot, and the first thing that I recollected was, that I was supported by Brothers Hyde and Russell, who were beseeching a throne of grace in my behalf. They then laid me on the bed, but my agony was so great that I could not endure, and I was obliged to get out, and fell on my knees and began to pray. I then sat on the bed and could distinctly see the evil spirits, who foamed and gnashed their teeth upon us. We gazed upon them about an hour and a half, and I shall never forget the horror and malignity depicted on the countenances of these foul spirits, and any attempt to paint the scene which then presented itself, or portray the malice and enmity depicted in their countenances would be vain.

I perspired exceedingly, and my clothes were as wet as if I had been taken out of the river. I felt exquisite pain, and was in the greatest distress for some time. However, I learned by it the power of the adversary, his enmity against the servants of God and got some understanding of the invisible world.

The Lord delivered us from the wrath of our spiritual enemies and blessed us exceedingly that day, and I had the pleasure (notwithstanding my weakness of body from the shock I had experienced) of baptizing nine individuals and hailing them brethren in the kingdom of God.

A circumstance took place while at the water side which I cannot refrain from mentioning, which will show the eagerness and anxiety of some in that land to obey the gospel. Two of the candidates who were changing their clothes and preparing for baptism at the distance of several rods from the place where I was standing in the water, were so anxious to obey the gospel, that they ran with all their might to the water, each wishing to be baptized first. The younger, being quicker on foot than the elder, out-ran him, and came first into the water. The circumstance reminded me of Peter and another disciple, who went to see the sepulchre where the Savior was laid: their anxiety was so great to find out whether He was yet there or not, that they had a race for it.

The ceremony of baptizing being somewhat novel, a large concourse of people assembled on the banks of the river to witness the ceremony.

In the afternoon, Elder Russell preached in the market-place, standing on a pedestal, to a very large congregation, numbers of whom were pricked to the heart.

Thus the work of the Lord commenced in that land (notwithstanding the rage of the adversary and his attempt to destroy us)—a work which shall roll forth, not only in that land but upon all the face of the earth, even "in lands and isles unknown."

The next morning we held a council, at which Elders Goodson and Richards were appointed to go to the city of Bedford, there being a good prospect, from the information received, of a Church being built up in that city. Elders Russell and Snider were appointed to go to Alston, in Cumberland, near the borders of Scotland, and Elders Hyde, Fielding and the writer were to remain in Preston and the regions round about.

The next day, the brethren took their departure for the different fields of labor assigned them.

Brothers Hyde, Fielding and I continued lifting up our voices in private houses, at the corners of the streets, in the market-place and wherever the Lord opened a door. The following Sabbath, Elder Hyde preached in the market-place to a numerous assemblage, both rich and poor, who flocked from all parts to hear "what these babblers had to say," hearing that we were "setters forth of strange doctrines." After Brother Hyde had got through, I gave an exhortation, and when I had concluded, a minister stepped forward to oppose us on the doctrines we advanced, but more particularly on the doctrine of baptism, he being a great stickler for infant baptism.

The people, thinking he intended to offend us, would not let him proceed, but seemed determined to put him down, and undoubtedly would have done so had not Brother Hyde interposed and begged permission for the gentleman to speak, telling the congregation that he was prepared to meet any arguments he might advance. This appeased the people, who listened to the remarks of the reverend gentleman; after which Brother Hyde spoke in answer to the objections which had been offered, to the satisfaction of nearly all present.

The minister felt somewhat ashamed. One individual came up to him and asked him what he now thought of his "baby baptism," while another came, took him by the hand and led him out of the throng. Indeed, all those who arose up to oppose the doctrines we taught were confounded, and could not with any success combat the truths we preached.

CHAPTER III

MEETING FOR CONFIRMATION — CONVERT AND BAPTIZE MISS
RICHARDS — HER FATHER, A MINISTER, INVITES ME TO PREACH
IN HIS CHAPEL — CONGREGATION BELIEVE MY TESTIMONY — MR.
RICHARDS FRIGHTENED — CLOSES HIS CHAPEL AGAINST ME —
HIS DAUGHTER TROUBLED — I PREDICT THAT HE WILL AGAIN
OPEN HIS CHAPEL TO ME — PREDICTION FULFILLED — OTHER
ELDERS ENCOURAGED BY THE REV. MR. MATTHEWS, WHO
AFTERWARDS REJECTS THEIR TESTIMONY AND COMMENCES
PREACHING THEIR DOCTRINES ON HIS OWN ACCOUNT.

Having had considerable success the short time we had labored in that place, and having baptized a number we requested them to meet at the house of Sister Dawson for confirmation on the evening of the second Sabbath after our arrival in Preston.

The people having come together, we fully explained to them the nature of that ordinance about to be performed. We then laid our hands upon between forty and fifty for the gift of the Holy Ghost, and confirmed them members of the Church of Jesus Christ of Latter-day Saints. While attending to this ordinance the Spirit of the Lord rested down upon us in a powerful manner, which caused us to rejoice exceedingly. Thus the word of the Lord spread and prevailed.

About this time, a young lady, the daughter of a minister of the Presbyterian order, who resided about fifteen miles from Preston, being on a visit to that place, happened to be at the house of a family with whom I was acquainted. Calling in to see them at the time she was there I was introduced to her, and we immediately entered into conversation on the subject of the gospel. I found her a very intelligent person, and she seemed very desirous to hear the things I had to teach and understand the doctrines of the gospel.

I informed her of an appointment I had made to preach that evening, and invited her to attend. She did so, and likewise the evening following; and after attending these two services she was fully convinced of the truth, and the next morning sent for me, desiring to be baptized. I cheerfully complied with her request, and confirmed her at the water side. The following day, she started for home, requesting me to pray for her, and gave us some encouragement to expect that her father would open his chapel for me to preach in.

I hastened to my brethren, told them of the circumstance and the result of my visit with the young lady, and then called upon them to unite in prayer that the Lord would soften the heart of her father, that he might be induced to open his chapel for us to preach in, and that our way might be opened in that place.

The next week I received a letter from her, and one from her father, in which he informed me that I was expected to be at his place the following Saturday, as he had given out an appointment for me to preach in his chapel the next Sunday. The following is a copy of the letter:

"*Sir*: — You are expected to be here next Saturday. You are given out to preach in the forenoon, afternoon and evening. Although we be strangers to one another, yet I hope we are not strangers to our blessed Redeemer, else I would not have given out for you to preach; our chapel is but little and the congregation but few — yet if one soul be converted, it is of more value than the whole world.

I remain in haste,

JOHN RICHARDS."

Agreeable to the kind invitation, I made preparation to visit that place, and took coach on Saturday afternoon at Preston and arrived at his house a little before dark.

On my entering, he arose and said, "I understand you are the minister lately from America!"

I told him I was, whereupon he bade me welcome to his house, and seemed to rejoice at my arrival.

After receiving refreshment at his hospitable board, we commenced a conversation which lasted till a late hour, which appeared satisfactory to the whole family.

The next morning I accompanied the reverend gentleman to his chapel, and at the hour appointed commenced to preach to a crowded congregation on the principles of salvation. I likewise preached in the afternoon and evening, and my hearers seemed to manifest great interest in the things which I laid before them. Nearly the whole congregation shed tears of joy.

After I had concluded the services of the day, Mr. Richards gave out another appointment for me to preach on Monday evening, which I attended to. I likewise, by request of the congregation, preached on Wednesday evening.

A number now began to believe the doctrines I advanced, and on Thursday, six individuals, all members of Mr. Richards' church, came forward for baptism.

Mr. Richards now, seeing the effect which my preaching produced, and fearing lest he should lose all his members and likewise the salary which was allowed him for preaching, told me that he must close the doors of his chapel against me; but at the same time his behavior was kind, and to his praise be it spoken, treated me with the greatest hospitality.

I then began to preach in private houses, which were opened in that neighborhood, and I ceased not to declare to all who came to hear, both by night and by day, the glorious tidings of salvation, and that God had again restored the ordinances as at the first, and counselors as at the beginning.

Notwithstanding Mr. Richards closed the door of his meeting house against me, he frequently came to hear me preach.

His daughter felt very sorrowful on account of her father not allowing me to preach any more in his place of worship, and wept much; but I told her not to fear, for I believed that God would soften his heart and cause him to open his chapel for me to preach in again.

During this time I was principally entertained at his house. The next Sunday I went along with him to his meeting, feeling a desire to hear him preach. After he had finished his discourse, I was surprised to hear him give out another appointment for me to preach in his chapel. I accordingly preached in the afternoon and in the evening, and the word seemed to be with power and the effect was great upon the people. The next day I baptized two more, both members of Mr. Richards' church.

Mr. Richards had preached in that place upwards of thirty years, and his members, as well as the inhabitants of the place and vicinity, were very much attached to him. Yet, when the fullness of the gospel was preached, although in much weakness, the people, notwithstanding their attachment and regard for their venerable pastor, being convinced of their duty, came forward and followed the footsteps of the Savior by being buried in the likeness of His death.

After laboring for some time in this neighborhood, I was warned by the Spirit to return to Preston, and there found that I was anxiously expected by the brethren. They had received letters from Brothers Richards and Russell, which gave an account of their proceedings since they left Preston. Brother Goodson had also returned from Bedfordshire, where he and Brother Richards had labored, and he gave us a relation of their mission and success.

He informed us that a minister by the name of Matthews, brother-in-law to Elder Joseph Fielding, received them very kindly and invited them to preach in his church. The invitation was accepted, and they preached several times. The result was that a number, among whom was Mr. Matthews and his lady, believed their testimony and the things which they proclaimed. Mr. Matthews had likewise borne testimony to his congregation of the truth of these things and that they were the same principles as taught by the apostles in ancient days, and beseeched his church to receive the same. Several of his members went forward and obeyed the gospel, and the time was appointed when he was to be baptized. However, in the interval, something had caused him to stumble, and darkness had pervaded his mind, insomuch so that at the time specified he did not make his appearance, but went to a Baptist minister residing in that place whom he prevailed upon to baptize him. From that time he began to preach baptism for the remission of sins, and no longer walked with the Saints. However, a great part of his members left him and obeyed the truth, and in a letter which he wrote to his brother-in-law, the Rev. James Fielding, he stated that his best members had left him.

It would probably be well to say a few words respecting Mr. Matthews and Mr. Fielding, and their congregations, also their situation prior to the time the gospel saluted their ears.

Mr. Matthews, who was a gentleman of considerable learning and talents, had been a minister in the established church of England. Seeing a great many things in that church contrary to truth and righteousness, and moreover, believing that an overturn was at hand, and that the church was destitute of the gifts of the Spirit, and was not expecting the Savior to come to reign upon the earth, as had been spoken by the prophets, he felt led to withdraw from that body.

He consequently gave up his prospects in that connection, and began to preach the things which he verily believed; and was instrumental in raising up quite a church in that place.

Mr. J. Fielding had been a minister in the Methodist church, but for some of the causes mentioned, had withdrawn from that society, and had collected a considerable church in Preston. Those gentlemen, with their congregations, were, I believe, diligently contending for that faith which was once delivered to the Saints at the time we arrived, but afterwards rejected the truth. Yet, notwithstanding they did not obey the gospel, the greater portion of their members received our testimony, obeyed the ordinances we taught, and are now rejoicing in the blessings of the new and everlasting covenant.

CHAPTER IV

THE PEOPLE EAGER TO HEAR US — WE RENT
"THE COCK PIT" TO PREACH IN — OBTAIN LICENSES
TO PREACH — CONTINUED SUCCESS.

About this time, Brother Snider returned from the north, where he had been laboring in company with Brother Russell. He stated that they had met with considerable opposition while preaching the gospel, but that some had obeyed the truth and that others were investigating.

After spending a few days with us, he and Brother Goodson took their leave of us and started for Liverpool about the first of October, on their way to America, having business of importance which called them home.

Although we were deprived of the labors of these brethren, the work of the Lord continued to roll forth with great power. The news of our arrival in that city, spread both far and wide, and calls from all quarters, to go and preach, were constantly sounding in our ears. We labored both night and day, that we might satisfy the people, who manifested such a desire for the truth as I never saw before.

We had to speak in small houses, to very large congregations, or else, to large assemblies in the open air; consequently, our lungs were very sore and our bodies considerably worn down with fatigue.

Soon after this, we obtained a large and commodious place to preach in, called "The Cock Pit," which had formerly been used by the people to witness cocks fight and kill one another, and where hundreds of spectators had shouted in honor of the barbarous sport which was once the pride of Britains. And now, instead of the huzzas of the wicked and profane, the gospel of Christ and the voice of praise and thanksgiving was heard there. The building had also been used for a temperance hall.

We had to pay seven shillings sterling per week for the use of it, and two shillings per week for the lighting, it being beautifully lit up with gas. It is situated in the center of the town, and about twenty rods from the "old church," probably the oldest in Lancashire. This church has twelve bells which are rung at every service, the noise of which was so great that we were unable to proceed in our services until they had done ringing them.

Our meeting was once disturbed by some ministers belonging to the Methodist church; however we got our place licensed and two gentlemen, who were constables, proffered their services to keep the peace and protect us from any further disturbances, which they continued to do, as long as we stayed in that land.

The effect of the gospel of Jesus Christ now began to be apparent, not only in the hearts of believers, but likewise in the conduct of those who rejected it and many began to threaten us with prosecution for preaching without having a license from the authorities of the nation.

This idea of obtaining a license from the secular authorities was somewhat novel to us, but after consulting our friends, among whom was Mr. Richards' son, (the minister of whom I have made mention) an attorney, practicing in that neighborhood, we found that it was according to the laws of the land.

Brother Hyde and I then made application to the quarter sessions for licenses and, by the assistance of Mr. Richards, obtained them.

Having now obeyed the requisitions of the law, we felt ourselves tolerably safe, knowing that our enemies now could not lawfully make us afraid or harm us.

Although we had many persecutors, who would have rejoiced at our destruction and who felt a determination to overthrow the work of the Lord, there were many who were very friendly, who would have stood by us under all circumstances, and would not have been afraid to hazard their lives in our behalf.

After we had labored for some time in Preston, and had baptized a number into the kingdom of God, Brother Hyde and I went about ten miles into the country to preach, agreeably to an invitation we had received. We preached twice to very numerous congregations, who paid great attention to our word, and who marveled at the things we proclaimed. We soon returned to Preston after which I paid a visit to the church at Walker Fold, that being the name of the place where the Rev. Mr. Richards resided. I found the church prospering, and after laboring a few days, several more were added. From that place I went to Bashe Lees, where I preached, and baptized two persons. I continued my journey thence to Ribchester, situated on the river Ribble, where I preached to a very large congregation, and then returned to Preston.

Having had some very pressing calls to go to some villages south of Preston, I accordingly started to visit those places, in company with Brother F. Moon, who had been baptized a short time previous. On arriving at our destination we gave out an appointment to preach, and, at the time appointed, the people flocked in crowds to hear me. Among the number were five preachers, who listened with great interest to my discourse, and who, with the greater part of the congregation, believed the doctrines I advanced.

The next day I went to a village called Askin, and preached in the evening; and the following day went to Eccleston, where I had the privilege of preaching in a Methodist chapel. The last three times I preached I baptized ten individuals, of whom two were preachers belonging to the Association Methodists.

After spending several days in that neighborhood I returned to Preston, where the church had now become numerous, and with the assistance of Elders Hyde and Fielding, proceeded to organize them. We divided the church into several branches, and appointed proper officers to preside over them.

Thursday evenings were appointed for prayer meetings to be held in different parts, and Sundays for the whole church to assemble in the Cock Pit, where the sacrament was administered, and such instructions given as were thought necessary for their spiritual prosperity and advantage.

While attending to this, the greatest harmony and love prevailed; and if ever any persons received the kingdom of heaven like little children it was those brethren.

After having attended to this duty, I again went into the country, where I spent the principal part of my time, occasionally visiting Preston.

During my labors, I was greatly assisted by the Spirit of the Lord, and my soul was comforted exceedingly. Churches were raised up in different directions, and many who had previously sat in darkness, upon them the true light shined, and before its benign and enlightening rays, the mists of darkness, the clouds of error and superstition fled; while "those who murmured learned doctrine, and those who erred in spirit came to understanding."

I was instrumental in building up churches in Eccleston, Wrightington, Askin, Exton, Daubers Lane, Chorly, Whittle and Laland Moss, after laboring about four weeks, and baptized upwards of one hundred persons, which caused me to rejoice exceedingly in the God and Rock of my salvation, that I had not to labor in vain, or spend my strength for nought. More loving and affectionate Saints I never saw before, and they were patterns of humility.

All the here-mentioned villages are within a very short distance of each other, and adjacent to Preston.

After my return from those places, I took a tour to the north-east of Preston in company with Elder Fielding, where we labored together a short time with considerable success, and raised up churches in Ribchester, Thomly, Soney Gate Lane and at Clitheroe, a very large market town, containing several thousand inhabitants.

At the latter place I baptized a preacher and six members of the Methodist church, immediately after I had preached the first time. We likewise baptized several in the town of Waddington and Downham.

The day after we preached in Downham, we received a very pressing invitation to preach in Chatburn, but having given out an appointment to preach in Clitheroe that evening, I informed those who had invited me that I would not be able to comply with their request. This did not satisfy them, and they continued to solicit me with the greatest importunity, until I was obliged to consent to go with them, after requesting Elder Fielding to attend to the other appointment.

On my arrival at the village I was cordially received by the inhabitants, who turned out in large numbers to hear me preach. I commenced my address to them in my usual manner, and the spirit of the Lord seemed to carry the word to the hearts of the congregation, who listened with great attention, and received the ingrafted word, which was able to make them wise unto salvation.

Being satisfied in my mind, from the witness of the spirit, that numbers were believing, I gave an opportunity to those who wished to obey the gospel to do so, and immediately repaired to the water, although it was late in the evening. Before I was done I baptized twenty-five for the remission of their sins, and was engaged in this pleasing duty until one o'clock, the next morning.

After being absent from Preston about seven days, in which time we had added eighty-three souls to the Church, we returned, praising God for all His mercies, and for visiting our labors with such abundant success.

> "No harvest joy can equal theirs
> Who see the fruit of all their cares."

CHAPTER V

It being near Christmas, we agreed to hold a general conference in Preston on Christmas day, there being business of importance to the churches to be attended to; and likewise several to be ordained to the ministry.

On Christmas day, the Saints assembled in the Cock Pit, and we then opened the conference, which was the first that was held by the Church of Christ in that country. There were about three hundred Saints present on the occasion, all of whom with the exception of three had been baptized within a very short time. Elders Hyde, Fielding and myself were present.

The brethren were instructed in the principles of the gospel, and their several duties enjoined upon them, as Saints of the Most High. We then proceeded to ordain several of the brethren to the Lesser Priesthood, to take charge of the different branches where they resided. We confirmed fourteen who had previously been baptized, and blessed about one hundred children.

At this conference, the Word of Wisdom was first publicly taught in that country; having previously taught it more by example than precept; and, from my own observation afterwards, I am happy to state that it was almost universally attended to by the brethren.

The Spirit of the Lord was with us during our interview, and truly the hearts of the Elders were rejoiced beyond measure when we contemplated the glorious work which had begun. We had to exclaim, "It is the Lord's doings, and it is marvelous in our eyes! Blessed be the name of the Lord!"

I felt greatly humbled before the Lord, who had crowned our labors with such signal success, and had prospered us far beyond my most sanguine expectations.

Immediately after this conference, Elder Hyde and I went to a village called Longton, situated near the sea-shore, where we raised the standard of truth, and published to the listening crowds, the glad tidings of salvation. After delivering two discourses, several came to us and requested baptism. It being very cold weather, insomuch that the streams were all frozen up, we had to repair to the sea-shore to administer that ordinance, and immersed fifteen in the waters of the ocean.

It would probably be too tedious, to enumerate all the particulars which occurred during the time we sojourned in that country; I shall therefore pass over many events which, though pleasing to us at that time, and which showed the kind dealings of our Heavenly Father, would not be sufficiently interesting to others. I shall therefore content myself by giving an outline of the principal circumstances attending our mission, which I have no doubt will be pleasing to the brethren, and to all who love the prosperity of Zion.

From this time, until about five weeks previous to our departure from that land, we were continually engaged in the work of the ministry, proclaiming the everlasting gospel in all the region round about, and baptizing all such as believed the gospel and repented of their sins. And truly, "the Lord of Hosts was with us, the God of Jacob was our refuge." The Holy Ghost the Comforter was given to us and abode with us in a remarkable manner, while the people thronged to hear our addresses, and "numbers were added to the church daily, such as should be saved." We would baptize as many as fifty in Preston in a week, exclusive of those in the country. During one short mission which Brother Hyde and I took into the country, after preaching five discourses on the principles of our holy religion, we had the pleasure of immersing one hundred and thirty in the waters of baptism.

Thus mightily ran the word of God and prospered to the joy and comfort of His servants, and to the salvation of precious and immortal souls; while the world was struck with amazement and surprise at the things which they saw and heard. During this state of things, our enemies were not idle, but heaped abuse upon us with an unsparing hand, and issued torrents of lies after us, which, however, I am thankful to say, did not sweep us away.

Among those most active in publishing falsehoods against us and the truth, were many of the reverend clergy, who were afraid to meet us face to face in honorable debate, although particularly requested so to do, but sought every opportunity to destroy our characters, and propagate their lies concerning us, thus giving testimony that "they loved darkness rather than light."

Although we frequently called upon the ministers of the different denominations, who had taken a stand against us, to come forward and investigate the subject of our religion before the world in an honorable manner, and bring forth their strong reasons to disprove the things we taught, and convince the people by sound argument and the word of God, if they could, that we did not preach the gospel of Christ, they altogether declined.

This course we felt moved upon by the Spirit to adopt; but they kept at a respectful distance, and only came out when we were absent, with misrepresentations and abuse. It is true we suffered some from the statements which they thought proper to make, when we could get no opportunity to contradict them; but generally their reports were of such a character that they carried along with them their own refutation.

The time when we expected to return to our native land, having now nearly arrived, it was thought necessary to spend the short time we had to remain in that country in visiting and organizing the churches; placing such officers over them, and giving such instructions as would be beneficial to them during our absence. Accordingly, Brothers Hyde, Fielding and I entered upon this duty, and we visited a Church nearly every day, and imparted such instructions as the Spirit directed. We first visited the Churches south of Preston, and after spending some time in that direction we journeyed to the north, accompanied by Brother Richards, who had just returned from the city of Bedford.

While we were attending to our duties in that section, we received a very pressing invitation from a Baptist church, through the medium of their deacon, to pay them a visit, stating that the society was exceedingly anxious to hear from our own lips, the wonderful things we had proclaimed in the regions round about.

We endeavored to excuse ourselves from going, as our engagements already were such that it would require the short time we had to stay to attend to them. But they seemed determined to take no denial, and plead with us with such earnestness that we could not resist their entreaties, and finally we consented to go and preach once.

Having arrived at the place, we found a large congregation already assembled in the Baptist chapel, anxiously awaiting our arrival. The minister gave out the hymns for us, and Elder Hyde spoke on the subject of the resurrection with great effect; after which the minister gave out another hymn which was sung by the assembly, and then he requested me to address them. I arose and spoke briefly on the first principles of the gospel.

During the services the congregation were overjoyed, the tears ran down their cheeks, and the minister could not refrain from frequently clapping his hands together for joy while in the meeting. After the service was over he took us to his house, where we were very kindly entertained.

After partaking of his hospitality he with some more friends, accompanied us to our lodgings, where we remained in conversation until a very late hour.

The next morning while we were preparing to depart we were waited upon by several of the citizens, who requested us to preach again that day, stating that great interest was felt by the inhabitants, many of whom were in tears, fearing they should hear us no more; and that a number of influential men, had suspended operations in their factories, to allow their workmen the privilege of hearing us preach. But we were obliged to deny them, as it was necessary to attend to the appointments we had previously made. We could scarcely tear ourselves away from them, and when we did so they wept like little children. Such a desire to hear the gospel, I never saw equalled before.

After commending them to the grace and mercy of God, we went to Downham, where we preached in the afternoon, after which forty came forward and were baptized. In the evening we called the churches of Chatburn and Downham together, and after confirming forty-five who had previously been baptized, we appointed priests, teachers and deacons to preside over them.

CHAPTER VI

IMPRESSED TO VISIT DOWNHAM AND CHATBURN—BAD CHARACTER OF THOSE PLACES—WARNED AGAINST GOING—JOY WITH WHICH THE GOSPEL WAS RECEIVED—THE PEOPLE EAGER TO BE BAPTIZED—LOTH TO PART WITH ME—VAIN OPPOSITION FROM A MINISTER—AFFECTING CONDUCT OF LITTLE CHILDREN.

There being something interesting in the establishing of the gospel in Downham and Chatburn, I will relate the circumstances of my visit to those places, and the prospect we had of success prior to our proclaiming the truth to them.

Having been preaching in the neighborhood of these villages, I felt it my duty to pay them a visit and tell them my mission. I mentioned my desires to several of the brethren, but they endeavored to dissuade me from going, informing me that there could be no prospect of success, as several ministers of different denominations had endeavored to raise churches in these places, and had frequently preached to them, but to no effect. They had resisted all the efforts and withstood the attempts of all sects and parties for thirty years, and the preachers had given them up to the hardness of their hearts. I was also informed that they were very wicked places and the inhabitants were hardened against the gospel.

However, this did not discourage me in the least, believing that the gospel of Jesus Christ could reach the heart when the gospels of men were found abortive. I consequently told those who tried to dissuade me from going that these were the places I wanted to go to, and that it was my business "not to call the righteous, but sinners to repentance."

Accordingly I went in the name of the Lord Jesus Christ, and I soon procured a large barn to preach in, which was crowded to excess. Having taken my stand in the middle of the congregation so that all might be able to hear, I commenced my discourse, spoke with great simplicity on the subject of the gospel of our Lord and Savior Jesus Christ, the conditions of pardon for a fallen world, and the privileges and blessings of all those who embraced the truth. I likewise said a little on the subject of the resurrection.

My remarks were accompanied by the spirit of the Lord and were received with joy, and these people, who were represented as being so hard and obdurate, were melted with tenderness and love, and such a feeling was produced as I never saw before; and the effect seemed to be general.

I then told them that, being a servant of the Lord Jesus Christ, I stood ready at all times to administer the ordinances of the gospel. After I had concluded, I felt some one pulling at my coat. I turned around and asked the person what it was he desired. The answer was "Please, sir, will you baptize me?" "and me!" "and me!" exclaimed more than a dozen voices.

We accordingly went down into the water, and before I left, I baptized twenty-five for the remission of sins—and was thus engaged until four o'clock the next morning.

Another evening the congregation was so numerous that I had to preach in the open air, and took my stand on a stone wall, and afterwards baptized a number.

These towns seemed to be affected from one end to the other; parents called their children together, spoke to them of the subjects upon which I had preached, and warned them against swearing and all other evil practices, and instructed them in their duty, etc. Such a scene I presume was never witnessed in this place before; the hearts of the people appeared to be broken, and the next morning they were all in tears, thinking they should see my face no more. When I left them my feelings were such as I cannot describe. As I walked down the street, followed by numbers, the doors were crowded by the inmates of the houses, waiting to bid us a last farewell, who could only give vent to their grief in sobs and broken accents.

While contemplating this scene we were induced to take off our hats, for we felt as if the place was holy ground. The Spirit of the Lord rested down upon us, and I was constrained to bless that whole region of country.

We were followed a considerable distance from the villages by a great number, who could hardly separate themselves from us. My heart was like unto theirs, and I almost thought my head was a fountain of tears, for I wept for several miles after I bid them adieu.

Some things transpired while I was in England which may be considered of but little importance by the world, but which will no doubt be appreciated by the Saints, who can not only mark the providence of God as displayed in nations and kingdoms, but can observe its workings in private life, and in affairs of but apparent small moment.

Soon after our arrival in England a great many of the "Aikenites" embraced the gospel, which caused considerable ill feeling and opposition among the ministers belonging to that sect.

Having lost quite a number, and seeing that many more were on the eve of being baptized, one of the ministers came to Preston and announced that he was going to put down "Mormonism," expose the doctrines and overthrow the Book of Mormon. He made a very long oration on the subject, and was very vehement in his manner, and pounded the Book of Mormon, which he held in his hand, on the pulpit a great many times. He then exhorted the people to pray that the Lord would drive us from their coasts, and if the Lord would not hear them in that petition, that he would smite the leaders.

The next Sunday Elder Hyde and I, being in Preston, went to our meeting and read the 13th chapter of Corinthians. We strongly urged upon the Saints the grace of charity, which is so highly spoken of in that chapter, and took the liberty of making some remarks on the proceedings of Mr. Aiken, the gentleman who had abused us and the Book of Mormon so very much a few days before. In return for his railing, we exhorted our people to pray that the Lord would soften his heart and open his eyes, that he might see that it was "hard to kick against the pricks."

The discourse had a very good effect, and that week we had the pleasure of baptizing about fifty into the kingdom of Jesus Christ, a large number of whom were members of Mr. Aiken's church.

Thus the Lord blessed us exceedingly, notwithstanding the railing and abuse of the priests, and all things worked together for our good and the advancement of the cause of truth.

I cannot refrain from relating a circumstance which took place, while Brother Fielding and I were passing through the village of Chatburn; having been observed drawing nigh to the town, the news ran from house to house, and immediately on our arrival, the noise of their looms was hushed, the people flocked to the doors to welcome us, and see us pass. The youth of the place ran to meet us, and took hold of our mantles and then of each other's hands. Several, having hold of hands, went before us, singing the songs of Zion, while their parents gazed upon the scene with delight, poured out their blessings upon our heads, and praised the God of heaven for sending us to unfold the principles of truth and the plan of salvation to them.

Such a scene, and such gratitude, I never witnessed before. "Surely," my heart exclaimed, "out of the mouths of babes and sucklings, thou has perfected praise!"

What could have been more pleasing and delightful than such a manifestation of gratitude to Almighty God from those whose hearts were deemed too hard to be penetrated by the gospel, and who had been considered the most wicked and hardened people in that region of country!

In comparison to the joy I then experienced, the grandeur, pomp and glory of the kingdoms of this world shrank into insignificance and appeared as dross, and all the honor of man, aside from the gospel, to be vain.

CHAPTER VII

VISIT TO THE MOON FAMILY—PREJUDICED AGAINST OUR
DOCTRINE—A PROPHECY ABOUT THEM—IMPRESSED TO CALL
AT THEIR HOUSE AGAIN—MY PRESENCE HAILED WITH JOY AS
AN ANSWER TO PRAYER—THE PROPHECY FULFILLED: THEY
JOIN THE CHURCH—A DREAM AND ITS INTERPRETATION.

Having an appointment to preach in the village of Wrightington, while on the way I stopped at the house of Brother Amos Fielding. When I arrived he informed me that a certain family by the name of Moon had sent a request by him for me to visit them, that they might have the privilege of conversing with me on the subject of the gospel. Accordingly, Brother Fielding and I paid them a visit that evening.

We were very kindly received by the family, and had considerable conversation on the object of my mission to that country, and the great work of the last days. They listened with attention to my statements, but they appeared to be prejudiced against them rather than otherwise. We remained in conversation until a late hour, and then returned.

On our way home, Brother Fielding observed that he thought our visit had been in vain, as the family seemed to have considerable prejudice. I replied, "Brother Fielding, be not faithless, but believing; we shall yet see great effects from this visit, for I know there are some of the family who have received the testimony and will shortly manifest the same."

At this remark he appeared surprised.

The next morning I continued my journey to Wrightington, and after spending two or three days in that vicinity, preaching the gospel, I returned by the way of Brother Fielding's, with whom I again tarried for the night.

The next morning I commenced my journey, intending to go direct to Preston, but when I got opposite the road leading to Mr. Moon's, I was forcibly impressed by the Spirit of the Lord to call and see them again. I could not resist, and therefore directed my steps to the house, not knowing what it meant.

On my arrival at the house, I knocked at the door, and Mrs. Moon from within exclaimed, "Come in! come in! you are welcome here! I and the lasses (meaning her daughters) have just been calling on the Lord, and praying that He would send you this way."

She then informed me of her state of mind since I was there before, and said she at first rejected my testimony, and endeavored to think lightly of the things I had advanced, but on trying to pray, she said that "the heavens seemed to be like brass over her head, and it was like iron under her feet." She did not know what was the matter, and exclaimed, "Certainly the man has not bewitched me!"

Upon inquiry she found it was the same with the "lasses." They had begun to reflect on the things I had told them, and, thinking it possible that I had told them the truth, they resolved to lay the case before the Lord, and beseech Him to give them a testimony concerning the things I had testified of.

She then observed, that as soon as they did so, light broke in upon their minds, they were convinced that I was a messenger of salvation, and that it was the work of the Lord; and they had resolved to obey the gospel, which they did, for that evening I baptized father and mother and four of their daughters.

Shortly after I visited them again, and baptized the remainder of the family, consisting of thirteen souls, the youngest of whom was over twenty years of age. They received the gospel as little children, and rejoiced exceedingly in its blessings. The sons were very good musicians, and the daughters excellent singers, and when they united their instruments and their voices in the songs of Zion, the effect was truly transporting.

Before I left England, there were about thirty of that family and connections baptized, six of whom were ordained to be fellow-laborers with us in the vineyard, and I left them rejoicing in the truths they had embraced.

One night, while at the village of Rochester, I dreamed that I, in company with another person, was walking out, and saw a very extensive field of wheat, more so than the eye could reach. Such a sight I never before witnessed. The wheat appeared to be perfectly ripe, and ready for harvest. I was very much rejoiced at the glorious sight which presented itself; but judge of my surprise, when, on taking some of the ears and rubbing them in my hands, I found nothing but smut. I marveled exceedingly, and felt very sorrowful, and exclaimed, "What will the people do for grain; here is a great appearance of plenty, but there is no sound wheat!"

While contemplating the subject, I looked in another direction, and saw a small field in the form of the letter L, which had the appearance of something growing in it. I immediately directed my steps to it, and found that it had been sown with wheat, some of which had grown about six inches high, other parts of the field not quite so high, and some had only just sprouted. This gave me great encouragement to expect that at the harvest there would be some good grain. While thus engaged, a large bull, very fierce and angry, leaped over the fence, ran through the field, and stamped down a large quantity of that which had just sprouted, and after doing considerable injury he leaped over the fence and ran away.

I felt very much grieved, that so much wheat should be destroyed, when there was such a prospect of scarcity. When I awoke next morning, the interpretation was given me. The large field with the great appearance of grain, so beautiful to look upon, represented the nation in which I then resided, which had a very pleasing appearance and a great show of religion, and made great pretensions to piety and godliness, but denied the power thereof. It was destitute of the principles of truth, and consequently of the gifts of the spirit.

The small field I saw clearly represented the region of country where I was laboring, and where the word of truth had taken root, and was growing in the hearts of those who had the gospel, some places having grown a little more than others. The village I was in, was that part of the field where the bull did so much injury, for during my short visit there, most of the inhabitants were believing, but as soon as I departed, a clergyman belonging to the church of England, came out and violently attacked the truth, and made considerable noise, crying, "false prophet! delusion!" and after trampling on truth, and doing all the mischief he could, before I returned, he took shelter in his pulpit. However, he did not destroy all the seed, for after my return I was instrumental in building up a church in that place.

CHAPTER VIII

EXTRAORDINARY SUCCESS—VERY COLD WEATHER—
SCENES OF SUFFERING—OUR EXCESSIVE LABORS—A GENERAL
CONFERENCE—FAREWELL MEETING—AFFECTION MANIFESTED
FOR US—ELDER RUSSELL'S LABORS—ELDER GOODSON A BARRIER.

It being known that we had but a short time to remain in that country, great numbers flocked to hear us preach, and many were baptized. Some days we went from house to house, conversing with the people on the things of the kingdom, and by such a course were instrumental in convincing many of the truth. I have known as many as twenty persons baptized in one day who have been convinced on such occasions. They were like Lydia of old, "who gladly received the word." I have had to go into the water to administer the ordinance of baptism six or seven times in a day, and frequently after having come out of the water and changed my clothes, I have had to return again before I reached my home; this, too, when the weather was extremely cold, the ice being from twelve to fourteen inches thick, which continued so about twelve weeks, during which time I think there were but ten days, in which we were not in the water. "The harvest was indeed plenteous but the laborers were few." This was very extraordinary weather for that country; as I was informed that some winters they had scarcely any frost or snow, and the oldest inhabitants told me that they never experienced such a winter before. In consequence of the inclemency of the weather, several manufacturing establishments were shut up, children were thrown out of employment, whose sufferings during that time were severe, and I was credibly informed, and verily believe, that numbers perished from starvation. Such sufferings I never witnessed in my life before, and the scenes which I daily beheld while in that country almost chilled the blood in my veins. The streets were crowded with men, women and children, who solicited alms from the passengers as they walked along. Numbers of those poor wretches were without shoes or stockings, and had scarcely any covering to screen them from the inclemency of the weather.

Oh! when will distress and poverty and pain cease, and peace and plenty abound? When the Lord Jesus shall descend in the clouds of heaven—when the rod of the oppressor shall be broken. "Hasten the time, O Lord!"

was frequently the language of my heart, when I contemplated the scenes of wretchedness and woe, which I daily witnessed, and my prayer to my Heavenly Father was, that if I had to witness a succession of such scenes of wretchedness and woe, that He would harden my heart, for those things were too much for me to bear. This is no exaggerated account; I have used no coloring here. They are facts which will meet the Elders of Israel when they shall go forth into that land, and then I can assure them they will not be surprised at my feelings.

But to return. During this time not only were great numbers initiated into the kingdom of heaven, but those who were sick were healed, and those who were diseased flocked to us daily; and truly their faith was great, such as I hardly ever witnessed before, consequently many were healed of their infirmities and sickness. We were continually employed, and scarcely gave sleep to our eyes, and some nights we would hardly close them. The task was almost more than we could endure, but realizing the circumstances of this people, their love of the truth, their humility and unfeigned charity, we were constrained to use all diligence and make good use of every moment of time, for truly our bowels yearned over them.

Notwithstanding our unwearied and unceasing labors, we could not fill the calls we had from day to day, for the work kept spreading, the prospect for usefulness grew brighter and brighter, and the field opened larger and larger.

The reader will not, I think, accuse me of egotism, when I say that we were diligent; for I do not remember of retiring to my bed earlier than twelve o'clock p. m. during the last six months I spent in that country, which was also the case with Brothers Hyde and Fielding. Brother Hyde was laid up with sickness about six weeks, on account of his excessive labors, from which however he was happily restored.

On the eighth day of April, A. D. 1838, it being Sunday, and the time appointed for a general conference of the Saints in that kingdom, and the day previous to our departure from them, they began to assemble at an early hour in the morning, and by nine o'clock there were from six to seven hundred of the Saints assembled from various parts of the country.

Believing it necessary for the good of the kingdom to have some one to preside over the whole mission, we nominated Brother Joseph Fielding to be appointed to that office, and Brother Levi Richards and William Clayton to be his counselors. The nominations met with the approbation of the whole assembly, who agreed to harken to their instructions and uphold them in their offices. These brethren were then, with eight Elders, several Priests, Teachers and Deacons, set apart and ordained to the several offices to which they were called. One of the brethren who was ordained was going to Manchester, one of the largest manufacturing towns in England, and another to the city of London, and they undoubtedly would carry the glad tidings of salvation to those places.

We then laid hands upon forty individuals, who had previously been baptized, for the gift of the Holy Ghost, after which about one hundred children were presented to us to receive a blessing, and the same day we baptized about twenty individuals for the remission of sins, and then proceeded to administer the sacrament to this numerous assembly. We then gave some general instructions to the whole Church respecting their duty to God and to one another, which were listened to with great attention and were treasured up in the hearts of most who were present.

At five o'clock, p. m., we brought the conference to a close, it having continued without intermission from nine o'clock, a. m. We then appointed seven o'clock the same evening to deliver our farewell addresses.

At the time appointed we repaired to the meeting, which was crowded to excess. Brother Hyde and myself then spoke to them respecting our labors in that land, the success of our ministry and the kindness we had experienced at their hands; told them that we hoped before long to see them again, after we had visited the Church and our families in America; but when we spoke of our departure their hearts were broken within them. They gave vent to their feelings and wept like children, and broke out in cries like the following: "How can we part with our beloved brethren!" "We may never see them again!" "O why can you leave us!" etc. I could not refrain; my feelings only found vent in a flood of tears.

Some persons may be disposed to accuse me of weakness on this occasion, but if any should do so, I would say that I do not envy any man's feelings who could witness such a scene with all its associations, and the finer feelings of his heart not be touched on such an occasion; indeed it would have been almost an impossibility for us to have left this dear and affectionate people had we not had the most implicit confidence in the brethren who were appointed to preside over them in our absence; but knowing their faith and virtuous conversation, and that they had the confidence of the Church, we felt assured that the affairs of the Church would be conducted in righteousness; consequently we left them under different feelings than we otherwise could have done.

Immediately after dismissing we met the official members, the number of whom were eighty, at a private house and instructed them further in their duties, and dismissed them at one o'clock the next morning.

This was certainly one of the most interesting conferences I ever attended. The services were calculated to convince the honest and give joy to Saints, and will long be remembered by all those who attended, and I have no doubt was the means of great and lasting good.

At this conference we were favored with the company of Elders Isaac Russell and Willard Richards. The latter had returned from the County of Bedford, where he had been proclaiming the gospel. In consequence of sickness his labors had not been so extensive as they otherwise would have been, and were confined within a short distance from the city of Bedford, where he raised up two small branches, which he set in order and ordained one Elder and other officers. He labored under considerable difficulty in consequence of the conduct of Elder Goodson, who accompanied him on that mission, who taught many things which were not in wisdom, which proved a barrier to the spread of the truth in that region. Elder Russell had returned from a mission to the north, having been laboring in the County of Cumberland, near the borders of Scotland, where numbers of his friends resided. While he was there he met with considerable opposition, even from those of his own family, as well as the ministers of the different denominations, who sought every opportunity to block up his way and to destroy his influence.

However, notwithstanding the great opposition, he was instrumental in bringing upwards of sixty souls into the kingdom of God, and left them rejoicing in the truth and strong in the faith of the gospel.

Thus the great work which is to go through the length and breadth of that land which will cause the hearts of thousands to rejoice, and the poor and meek to increase their joy in the Lord; which shall lead the honest-hearted to the foundation of truth; which shall prepare a holy company from that nation to meet the Lord Jesus when He shall descend from the mansions of glory and from the regions that are not known; which shall cause thousands to rail against the doctrines of Christ and His servants, and persecute the honest-in-heart; which shall prepare the ungodly for the day of vengeance of our God, and shall bind them together in the cords of darkness, was commenced in three places, viz: Preston, Bedford and Alston, which forcibly reminds me of the parable of the leaven which the woman cast into the three measures of meal.

CHAPTER IX

OUR LODGINGS — WANTS SUPPLIED BY LIBERALITY OF
SAINTS — JOURNEY TO LIVERPOOL — CONTRAST BETWEEN
ARRIVAL AND DEPARTURE — RETURN VOYAGE — MEETING WITH
ELDERS AND SAINTS AT NEW YORK — ARRIVAL AT KIRTLAND.

During our stay in Preston, we made our home at the house of Sister Dawson, in Pole Street. We purchased our provisions, and she cooked them for us, which is quite customary in that country. For our room, lodging and cooking and a good coal fire, we each paid the sum of two shillings sterling per week, which is but little more than half the usual charge. Sister Dawson was very kind to us. Indeed the hearts of all the Saints were open to liberality, and according to their circumstances they contributed liberally of their substance, and many blessings of a temporal nature we received from them, for which I pray that my Heavenly Father may reward them a hundred fold in this world, and in the world to come with life everlasting.

During the time we labored in England, we made no public contributions except for the poor. When we were about taking our departure, the Church, knowing that we had no means to carry us to our native land, with a liberality characteristic of them, contributed to our necessities and provided us with means to take us as far as Kirtland, Ohio. The next day, being the ninth of April, we engaged our passage to Liverpool in a coach, which was to start at twelve o'clock the same day. At the time appointed we were at the place of starting, and were soon surrounded with the brethren, who felt determined to see us leave, many of whose countenances clearly showed their sorrow at our departure. However, we had to bid them farewell, and were soon out of sight. Their eyes followed us as long as they could see us.

Notwithstanding the variegated scenery of the country, which in England is very beautiful, my mind reverted back to the time when I first arrived in that country, and the peculiar feelings I had when I traveled from Liverpool to Preston some months before. Then I was a stranger in a strange land, and had nothing to rely upon but the kindness and mercy of that God who had sent me there. While I mused on these things my soul was humbled within me, and I had to exclaim, "Surely this is the Lord's doings, and marvelous in my eyes!" for then I had hundreds of brethren to whom I was united in bonds the most endearing and sacred, and who loved me as their own souls, and whose prayers would be continually offered up for my welfare and prosperity.

After a ride of about four hours, we arrived at Liverpool and ascertained that the ship in which we intended to sail would not leave that port as early as we expected, in consequence of a great storm which had taken place, in which several vessels had been wrecked and a number of lives lost. We took lodgings a few days until the vessels should depart.

While in Liverpool, we were waited upon by Elders Fielding and Richards, who, feeling desirous to obtain all the information they could procure respecting the government of the church, thought that it would be a favorable time to do so, as our opportunities of instruction had been but limited while in Preston, and it being almost impossible to have much private intercourse, there being so many who wished to converse with us on the subject of the gospel, etc. But in this thing they were disappointed, for as soon as it was known in Preston and regions round about that our departure was delayed, numbers of the brethren came from thence to visit us in Liverpool before we left their shores.

On the 20th, we went on board the ship *Garrick* (the same ship in which we came), bound for New York, and the same day got under way. Soon after we left Liverpool a great storm came on, with a head wind, and continued without cessation for several days, which did considerable damage to the vessel. The bowsprit was broken twice by the force of the wind with only the gib sail set. The boom likewise came down with great force near the place where the captain was standing, but he fortunately escaped without injury. Several other parts of the rigging were much torn and injured. During the time the storm lasted, Brothers Hyde and Russell were very sick. After this we had more favorable weather.

When we had been on the water two weeks, I asked permission of the captain for one of us to preach, which request was cheerfully complied with, and the second cabin was prepared for the occasion. Brother Russell preached, after which Brother Hyde made some observations. The discourses were listened to with great attention, and the congregation appeared very much satisfied.

The Lord gave us favor in the eyes of the captain and the passengers, who treated us with respect and kindness. Those who were in the same cabin with ourselves, and with whom we had more frequent opportunities of conversing, treated us like brothers, and took pleasure in administering to our wants, and told us if they had anything we needed it was at our service. I hardly ever remembered traveling with more agreeable or kind-hearted people, and I pray that the Lord may bless them abundantly and reward them a hundred fold for all the kindness shown to His servants.

Nothing very particular occurred during the remainder of the passage. The weather for the most part was favorable. On the twelfth day of May we came in sight of New York, and in the evening we secured a landing, after a passage of twenty-two and one-half days. The ship *New England*, which left Liverpool on the same day we did, came in about one hour afterwards.

The sight of my native land filled my soul with gladness. We then went into the city with several of the passengers, who purchased some refreshments, and after we returned bade us partake with them, and we rejoiced together. We then bowed before the Lord and offered up the gratitude of our hearts for all His mercies, in prospering us in our mission and bringing us safely across the mighty deep, to behold once more the land of our nativity, and the prospect of soon embracing our families and friends.

The next morning we went in search of Brother Fordham, whom we found after some trouble. He was rejoiced to see us and immediately took us to the house of Brother Mace, where we were glad to see our beloved Brother Orson Pratt, who was then laboring in that city, and who with Elder Parley P. Pratt, his brother, had been instrumental in bringing many into the kingdom in that city, which intelligence gave us great joy, for when we left New York for England, there was only one belonging to the church in that city.

It being Sunday, we accompanied the Brothers Pratt to the house where the Saints were accustomed to assemble for worship. On entering the house we found about eighty persons assembled, all of whom had recently joined the Church. After singing and prayer, I was requested to give an account of our mission to England. I accordingly arose and told them the things which had happened to us since our departure, and the great and glorious work which our Heavenly Father had commenced on the islands of the sea, and the great desire of the English to hear the things which the Lord had brought to pass on this continent, and their ready reception of the truth of the gospel.

The information gave great joy to the Saints, and they united with us in praising the name of the Lord for His wonderful works for the children of men.

In the evening Elders Russell and Hyde preached, and a great effect was produced, and some came forward and offered themselves as candidates for baptism.

The short time we were in New York was spent very agreeably with the Saints, who were indeed a kind and affectionate people. The next day we bade adieu to the brethren and commenced our journey to Kirtland by steamboat and railroad, and arrived there on the twenty-second day of May, A. D 1838, having been absent eleven months and nine days.

CHAPTER X

REMOVAL TO MISSOURI—SICKNESS—KINDNESS OF THE
SAINTS AT FAR WEST—BUILD A HOUSE, AND THEN HAVE TO
ABANDON IT—BATTLE OF CROOKED RIVER—DEATH AND FINAL
TESTIMONY OF APOSTLE DAVID W. PATTEN—CORNER STONE
OF TEMPLE AT FAR WEST LAID—REMOVAL TO ILLINOIS.

I found my family in good health, and as comfortably situated as I could expect; and our joy was mutual. The Saints in Kirtland also received us with joy and welcomed us home.

But my journey was not yet ended. Soon after my arrival in Kirtland, I had to make preparation to move to the State of Missouri, where the greater part of the Church had already gone. One great cause of their removal to the west, was the persecutions to which they were subject in Kirtland. The brethren who yet resided there, although very kind and affectionate, were weak in the faith in consequence of trials and temptations. This caused us to grieve exceedingly, and we resolved to cheer them up as much as we possibly could.

Being solicited to preach in the house or the Lord, we did so, and after preaching a few times, and recounting our travels and the great success which had attended our labors, and also the marvelous work which the Lord had commenced and was still carrying on in the old country, they began to take courage, their confidence increased, and their faith was strengthened, and they again realized the blessings of Jehovah.

As soon as our circumstances would permit, we commenced our journey to the State of Missouri, by water, a distance of nearly eighteen hundred miles. After enduring considerable fatigue, we arrived safely at Far West, on the 25th of July. We had the pleasure of beholding the faces of numbers of our friends and brethren, some of whom were so glad to see us that tears started in their eyes when we took them by the hand.

There is indeed something peculiarly pleasing to the Saint, who, after a long separation, beholds the friends to whom he is united in bonds the most sacred, and with whom he has probably traveled to preach the gospel, and with them passed through many scenes of sorrow and affliction. At that time every pleasing association is revived, and memory fondly clings to those scenes, the contemplation of which affords pleasure, while every thing of an opposite nature is forgotten and buried in oblivion.

During our journey from Kirtland to Missouri, the weather was remarkably warm, in consequence of which I suffered very much, and my body was broken down by sickness, and I continued very feeble for a considerable length of time.

The first Sunday after my arrival at Far West I was called upon to preach to the Saints, which I endeavored to do, although I was scarcely able to stand. I related many things respecting my mission and travels, which were gladly received by the brethren, whose hearts were cheered by the recital, while many of the Elders were stirred up to diligence, and expressed a great desire to accompany us when we should return to England.

Soon after my arrival, I had a lot given me by Bishop Partridge, and also sufficient timber to build me a house. While it was being erected, I lived in a place I built for my cow, about eleven feet square, and in which I could hardly stand upright. The brethren were remarkably kind and contributed to my necessities. One of them by the name of Charles Hubbard, made me a present of forty acres of land, another gave me a cow, etc.

When I had nearly finished my house, and after much labor, I was obliged to abandon it to the mob, who at that time commenced persecuting the Saints, driving off their cattle and destroying their property.

It will not be expected that I should recapitulate the circumstances which then transpired, which were of an extraordinary character, as numbers have written on the subject. Suffice it to say, that the Saints suffered privations, hunger, abuse, cold, famine, and many of them death. Yes, the blood of the Saints has stained the soil of Missouri, for which the King of kings and Lord of hosts will recompense upon her the punishment of her crimes.

From about the 6th of August until the 1st of November it was a continual scene of agitation and alarm, both by night and by day. The enemies of righteousness were determined to overthrow the Saints, and, regardless of all laws (which were trampled upon with impunity), they made every preparation, and used every means in their power to accomplish their unhallowed designs.

The Saints, tenacious of their liberties and sacred rights, resisted these unlawful designs, and with courage worthy of them, they guarded their families and their homes from the aggressions of the mob, but not without the loss of several lives, among whom was my greatly esteemed and much lamented friend, Elder David W. Patten, who fell a sacrifice to the fell spirit of persecution, and a martyr to the cause of truth. The circumstances of his death I will briefly relate:

It being ascertained that a mob had collected on Crooked River, in the County of Caldwell, a company of sixty or seventy persons immediately volunteered from Far West to watch their movements and repel their attacks, and chose Elder Patten for their commander. They commenced their march about midnight and came up to the mob very early next morning, and as soon as the brethren approached near to them, they were fired upon, when Captain Patten received a shot which proved fatal. The mob after firing ran away. Several others of the brethren were wounded at the same time, some of whom afterwards died.

Immediately on receiving the intelligence that Brother Patten was wounded, I hastened to see him. When I arrived he appeared to be in great pain, but still was glad to see me. He was conveyed about four miles to the house of Brother Winchester. During his removal his sufferings were so excruciating, that he frequently desired us to lay him down that he might die. But being desirous to get him out of the reach of the mob and among friends, we prevailed upon him to let us convey him there.

He lived about an hour after his arrival, and was perfectly sensible and collected until he breathed his last. He had medical assistance, yet his wound was such that there was no hope entertained of his recovery. This he was perfectly aware of. In this situation, while the shades of time were lowering and eternity with all its realities was opening to his view, he bore a strong testimony to the truth of the work of the Lord and the religion he had espoused.

The principles of the gospel which were so precious to him before, were honorably maintained in nature's final hour, and afforded him that support and consolation at the time of his departure which deprived death of its sting and its horror.

Speaking of those who had fallen from their steadfastness, he exclaimed, "O that they were in my situation; for I feel that I have kept the faith; I have finished my course; henceforth there is laid up for me a crown which the Lord, the righteous Judge, shall give to me," etc.

Speaking to his beloved partner, who was present, and who attended him in his dying moments, he said, "Whatever you do else, O, do not deny the faith!" He all the while expressed a great desire to depart. I spoke to him and said, "Brother David, when you get home I want you to remember me." He immediately exclaimed, "I will." At this time his sight was gone.

We felt so very much attached to our beloved brother, that we beseeched the Lord to spare his life and endeavored to exercise faith in the Lord for his recovery. Of this he was perfectly aware, and expressed a wish that we should let him go, as his desire was to be with Christ.

A few minutes before he died he prayed as follows: "Father, I ask thee, in the name of Jesus Christ, that thou wouldst release my spirit and receive it unto Thyself!" and then said to those who surrounded his dying bed, "Brethren, you have held me by your faith, but do give me up, and let me go, I beseech you."

We then committed him to God, and he soon breathed his last, and slept in Jesus without a groan.

This was the end of one who was an honor to the Church and a blessing to the Saints, and whose faith and virtues and diligence in the cause of truth will be long remembered by all who had the pleasure of his acquaintance; and his memory will be had in remembrance by the Church of Christ from generation to generation.

It was indeed a painful circumstance to be deprived of the labors of this worthy servant of Christ, and it east a gloom over the Saints; yet the glorious and sealing testimony which he bore of his acceptance with heaven, and the truth of the gospel, was a matter of joy and satisfaction, not only to his immediate friends, but to the Saints at large.

I remained in the State of Missouri until the 26th of April, A. D. 1839, it being the time appointed by revelation for the Twelve to take their leave of the building spot of the house of the Lord and take their journey across the ocean, and notwithstanding the threats of our enemies that this prophecy should fail, we assembled on the public square, at Far West, assisted Elder Alpheus Cutler to lay the corner foundation stone, sang a hymn and united in prayer to God that He would give us a prosperous mission.

During my stay in Missouri, I frequently went to see the brethren who were confined in prison for the testimony of Jesus and for the word of God. Many times after I had traveled forty or fifty miles to see them, I was denied the privilege by the jailor and the guards.

I was with the brethren in nearly all their movements in the west, and can bear testimony to their faith and virtues, and know they were entirely innocent of the crimes alleged against them, and that their persecutions were brought upon them on account of their attachment to the gospel and to the Saints of the Lord.

Although they were in the Lands of their enemies, who threatened to kill them, I always had the testimony that they would be delivered and come forth victorious.

After the 26th of April, A. D. 1839, I took leave of Far West, and in company with my brethren traveled to Illinois, where my family had removed some time previous, and I had the unspeakable pleasure of seeing my beloved friends, the First Presidency and others who had been delivered out of the hands of their enemies and had arrived safely in Illinois.

Soon after a general conference of the Church was held near Quincy, at which the Saints from all the regions round about assembled. It was a time which will long be remembered by the Saints, it being the first conference held after their expulsion.

CHAPTER XI

FAR WEST BESIEGED—JOSEPH SMITH AND
BRETHREN BETRAYED BY APOSTATES—ATROCITIES
OF MOB—CONVERSATION WITH W. E. M'LELLIN—
EXTERMINATION SPEECH OF GENERAL CLARK.

Before I proceed farther with my narrative, it may perhaps be as well to revert to some other things that transpired in Missouri:

After witnessing the death of D. W. Patten, I took Dr. Avard with me to Far West, a distance of three miles, to Elder Rigdon's house, where we found Brother Patrick O'Banion, who was shot in nearly the same place as Brother Patten (he was a member of Zion's Camp in 1834). He also died in a short time, firm and steadfast in the faith, was perfectly calm and composed, and bore a strong testimony to the truth of "Mormonism."

Gideon Carter, who was also a faithful Saint, was shot in the head and left dead on the ground, so defaced that the brethren did not at first know him.

This was a gloomy time!

On the 30th of October, 1838, we discovered several thousand of the mob coming to Far West, under pretense of being government troops. They passed through our corn and wheat fields, making a complete desolation of every thing in their way.

Brother Brigham Young and I were appointed captains of fifty, in a hurry, and commanded to take our position right in the thoroughfare on which the mob were seen advancing to the city, momentarily anticipating the awful tragedy of a bloody massacre. Joseph was with us, giving counsel.

The army came up to good rifle shot distance and halted. Seeing our temporary fortifications, which we had thrown up the night previous, by pulling down some of our houses, and fixing up our wagon, they dared not approach nearer, but retreated back to Goose Creek, about three-fourths of a mile, screaming, hallooing and screeching. The mob afterwards declared there were fifteen hundred of us stationed there to prevent their approach, but to my certain knowledge there were only about one hundred and fifty in that line.

The word came that Joseph Smith and several others were to be given up; otherwise the mob would massacre every man, woman and child.

In order to prevent the execution of this threat, Joseph gave himself up, with Elders Sidney Rigdon, P. P. Pratt, Lyman Wight and George W. Robinson, they having been betrayed into the camp by Col. George M. Hinkle and other apostates.

On the 1st of November, the mob, professing to be the regular militia of the State of Missouri, numbering about seven thousand, surrounded Far West. Our men were all taken prisoners and then marched a short distance into a hollow, where Col. Lucas had previously pointed his cannon in full range, so that if we failed to lay down our arms, he could easily sweep us into eternity, which was his design. We were then formed into a hollow square and commanded by Col. Lucas to ground arms and deliver up our weapons of war, although they were our own private property. After being marched back a short distance, on the public square, we were again formed into a hollow square, near the house of Widow Beeman.

The mob commenced plundering the citizens of their bedding, money, wearing apparel and everything of value they could lay their hands upon. Much property was destroyed by the burning of houses, logs, rails, corn cribs, boards, etc., the using of corn and hay, the killing of cattle, sheep and hogs, etc., and all this without regard to owners, or asking leave of any one. In the meantime, men were abused, and women insulted, and treated with violence by the troops, while the men were kept prisoners.

We were compelled at the point of the bayonet to sign a deed of trust for the purpose of making our individual property liable, as they said, to pay all the debts of persons belonging to the Church, and also for all damages the old inhabitants of Daviess County might have sustained in consequence of the late difficulties in that County.

When General Clark arrived, the first important move made by him, was collecting our men together on the square, and selecting about fifty of them, whom he immediately marched into a house and confined closely. This was done without the aid of the sheriff or any legal process.

The next day, forty-six of those taken, with the Prophet Joseph, were driven, like a parcel of menial slaves, off to Richmond, not knowing why they were taken.

When these troops surrounded us, and we were brought into a hollow square, the first persons that I knew, were men who had once professed to be our brethren. They were the men who piloted the mob into our city, namely: William E. McLellin and Lyman E. Johnson, two of the Twelve; John Whitmer and David Whitmer, two of the witnesses to the Book of Mormon; William W. Phelps, and scores of others, "hail fellows, well met."

A portion of the troops were painted like Indians, and looked horrible. They were led by Niel Gillum, who styled himself "the Delaware chief," who, with many others, cocked his gun upon us and swore he would blow our brains out, although we were disarmed and helpless.

William E. McLellin inquired where Heber C. Kimball was, and some one pointed me out to him. I was sitting on the ground. When he came up to me, he said, "Brother Heber, what do you think of Joseph Smith, the fallen prophet, now? Has he not led you blindfolded long enough? Look and see yourself poor, your family stripped and robbed, and your brethren in the same fix. Are you not satisfied with Joseph?"

I replied, "Yes, I am more satisfied a hundred fold than I was before; for I see you in the very position that he foretold you would be in — a Judas to betray your brethren, if you did not forsake your adultery, fornication, lying and abominations. Where are you? What are you about — you, and Hinkle, and scores of others? Have you not betrayed Joseph and his brethren into the hands of the mob, as Judas did Jesus? Yes, verily, you have! I tell you 'Mormonism' is true, and Joseph is a true Prophet of the living God, and you with all others that turn therefrom will be damned and go to hell, and Judas will rule over you!"

Soon after this, when things began to be a little more quiet, I desired to go to my home to get something to eat, many of us not having eaten any food for twenty-four hours. I asked some of the mob standing near if I could have the privilege of going to my house, a little distance off. They referred me to their captain, who was Bogart, the Methodist preacher. I went to him and told him what I wanted. He first spoke of sending some one with me, as I would be liable to be shot if found alone. In a short time, however, he said, "I will go with you."

He went down to my house, and my wife got some dinner and he ate with me; then we returned, and I again took my seat on the ground with my brethren who were under guard.

The next day I was permitted to return to my home, but told that I need not try to leave the city as it was surrounded with a strong guard to prohibit any one leaving the place. The mob were engaged taking every man a prisoner who seemed to have any influence, and putting him in chains to await a trial.

It was rumored that all the men who were in the Crooked River battle would be taken prisoners; therefore, many of them fled to the north before the guards were placed around the city.

The 6th of November, General Clark delivered his noted extermination speech, and read over the names of fifty-six brethren who were made prisoners, to await a trial for something they knew not what.

In order that the tyrant may not be forgotten, I insert a portion of his speech:

"GENTLEMEN: — You whose names are not attached to this list of names, will now have the privilege of going to your fields, and of providing corn, wood, etc., for your families. Those who are now taken will go from this to prison, be tried and receive the due demerit of their crimes; but you, (except such as charges may hereafter be preferred against,) are at liberty, as soon as the troops are removed that now guard the place, which I shall cause to be done immediately. It now devolves upon you to fulfil a treaty that you have entered into, the leading items of which I shall now lay before you. The first requires that your leading men be given up to be tried according to law; this you already have complied with. The second is, that you deliver up your arms; this has been attended to. The third stipulation is that you sign over your properties to defray the expenses of the war. This you have also done. Another article yet remains for you to comply with — and that is, that you leave the State forth with. And whatever may be your feelings concerning this, or whatever your innocence, it is nothing to me. General Lucas (whose military rank is equal with mine,) has made this treaty with you; I approve of it. I should have done the same had I been here. I am therefore determined to see it executed. The character of this State has suffered almost beyond redemption, from the character, conduct and influence that you have exerted; and we deem it an act of justice to restore her character to its former standing among the States by every proper means. The orders of the governor to me were, *that you should be exterminated, and not allowed to remain in the State*. And had not your leaders been given up, and the terms of the treaty complied with, before this time you and your families would have been destroyed, and your houses in ashes. There is a discretionary power vested in my hands, which, considering your circumstances, I shall exercise for a season. You are indebted to me for this clemency. I do not say that you shall go now, but you must not think of staying here another season or of putting in crops; for the moment you do this the citizens will be upon you; and if I am called here again in case of non-compliance of a treaty made, do not think that I shall do as I have done now. You need not expect any mercy, but *extermination, for I am determined the governor's order shall be executed*. As for your leaders, do not think, do not imagine for a moment, do not let it enter into your minds, that they will be delivered and restored to you again, for *their fate is fixed, their die is cast, their doom is sealed.* I am sorry, gentlemen, to see so many apparently intelligent men found in the situation that you are; and oh! if I could invoke that Great Spirit, THE UNKNOWN GOD, to rest upon and deliver you from that awful chain of superstition, and liberate you from those fetters of fanaticism with which you are bound — that you no longer do homage to a man. I would advise you to scatter abroad, and never again organize yourselves with Bishops, Presidents, etc., lest you excite the jealousies of the people and subject yourselves to the same calamities that have now come upon you. You have always been the aggressors — you have brought upon yourselves these difficulties, by being disaffected, and not being subject to rule. And my advice is, that you become as other citizens, least by a recurrence of these events you bring upon yourselves irretrievable ruin."

He also said, "You must not be seen as many as five together; if you are, the citizens will be upon you and destroy you, but you should flee immediately out of the State. There is no alternative for you but to flee; you need not expect any redress; there is none for you."

I was present when that speech was delivered, and I can truly say that he is a liar and the truth is not in him, for not one of us had made any such agreement with Lucas, or any other person. What we did was by compulsion in every sense of the word; and as for General Clark and his unknown god, they had nothing to do with our deliverance; but it was our Father in heaven, the God of Abraham, of Isaac and of Jacob, in whom we trust, who liveth and dwelleth in the heavens; and the day will come when our God will hold him in derision, with all of his coadjutors.

CHAPTER XII

PERILS OF THE PEOPLE — CHEERFULNESS OF THE
SAINTS AMIDST THEIR TROUBLES — VISIT OUR BRETHREN
IN PRISON — APOSTLES ORDAINED — MOCK DISTRIBUTION
OF STATE APPROPRIATION — LETTER FROM JOSEPH SMITH
AND BRETHREN IN PRISON — INDIFFERENCE OF STATE
OFFICIALS TO OUR APPEALS — WORD OF THE LORD TO ME.

One afternoon, I sent my son William a short distance on an errand, when, on his return, one of the guards drew up his rifle and threatened to blow out his brains if he stepped one inch further towards the house. Through the agency of some of my brethren, I was notified of it. I went to the man and spoke to him in a friendly manner, and conversed with him about the beautiful country, it being more beautiful than England and the nations I had been traveling in.

He became very much interested, and in a short time I pointed out my son William, who had stood still for some time after being warned not to approach, and was cold, as it was then dusk and the weather severe. Said I, "That is my son."

"Oh!" he said, "if that is one of your sons, he may pass; he may go home."

Afterwards the man left his post and came to my house and spent the evening and several times afterwards, and became very friendly, and told me he wished I would leave the "Mormons," as he liked me, and could not bear the thought of my following them with my family, for we were too good for them.

I merely mention this to show the perils we were in, men, women and children, with death and destruction waiting on us, and this spirit aroused by apostates.

The murders, house burnings, robberies, rapes, drivings, whippings, imprisonments, chainings and other sufferings and cruelties inflicted upon the people of God under illegal orders of Missouri's executive, have been only in part laid before the world, and form a page in history unparalleled in the records of religious persecution. This historic page alone can credit Lilburn

W. Boggs and his minions with feeding the ministers of the proscribed religion on the flesh of their murdered brethren, the odium of which crime is shared fully by the professed ministers of different denominations who participated in these vile atrocities! If hell can furnish a parallel, where is it?

For me to undertake to write what I saw, and felt and realized, I should utterly fail for lack of ability; I must let eternity reveal the scenes of those days. I can say before God, angels, heaven and earth, that I am innocent of violating any law of the State of Missouri, and I can say that my brethren are as pure and clean as I am, innocent and virtuous, true to their God and their country. With the measure they meted to the Latter-day Saints, it shall be measured to them again, or upon all those who had a hand in our persecution and expulsion, and those who consented to it, four fold, full, pressed down, and running over shall be their portion; and as the Lord God Almighty liveth, I shall live to see it come to pass. [A]

[Footnote A: Elder Kimball lived to see the fulfillment of this prophecy.]

When we walked up to sign the deeds of trust to pay these assassins for murdering our brethren and sisters and their children, ravishing some of our sisters to death, robbing us of our lands and possessions and all we had on earth, and other such *services*, they expected to see us cast down and sorrowful; but I testify as an eye-witness that the brethren rejoiced and praised the Lord and kicked up their heels, and thanked God, taking joyfully the despoiling of their goods. There were judges, magistrates and Methodist, Presbyterian, Campbellite and other sectarian priests who stood by and saw all this going on, exulting over us, and it seemed to make them more angry that we bore our misfortunes so cheerfully. Judge Cameron said, with an oath, "See them creatures laugh and kick up their heels! They are whipped but not conquered."

I have no doubt that I would have been taken a prisoner had the mob known me, but I had not been there but three weeks when the mobbing commenced, and was only known by the brethren, and many of them I had not seen during my brief residence there. The mob had not become acquainted with Brother Brigham, either, as he lived three or four miles from the city on Mill Creek.

After the mob departed, I accompanied Brother Brigham to Richmond jail to see our brethren. We found Joseph, Hyrum, Sidney and others chained together in one room, and others confined in other places among the worst demons living out of hell. We scarcely had the privilege of speaking to our brethren more than to say, "How do you do?" every eye being upon us with suspicion. We put up at a public house for the night, and I bear testimony, from our feelings and the spirit manifested in that house, that there were legions of devils present. I do not think that either of us slept any that night.

On the 13th of December, Elder Brigham Young and I reorganized the High Council at Far West, when we expressed our fellowship with all those who desired to do right, and filled the vacancies occasioned by those brethren who had to flee from Missouri to save their lives.

On the 19th of December, 1838, Brother Brigham and I ordained Elders John Taylor and John E. Page Apostles.

The legislature of the State of Missouri appropriated two thousand dollars, to be distributed among the people of Daviess and Caldwell Counties, the "Mormons" not excepted. Judge Cameron, Mr. McHenry and others attended to the distribution. Judge Cameron drove in the hogs belonging to the brethren (many of which were identified), shot them down in the street, and without further bleeding, they were half dressed, cut up and distributed by Mr. McHenry to the poor, at the rate of four and five cents per pound, which, together with a few pieces of refuse calicoes at double and treble prices, soon consumed the appropriation.

I received the following letter from the Prophet and his brethren while they were in prison.

"LIBERTY,

"Jan. 16th, 1839.

"BROTHERS H. C. KIMBALL AND B. YOUNG:

"*Joseph Smith, Jun., Sidney Rigdon and Hyrum Smith, prisoners for Jesus' sake, send greeting*: — In obedience to your request in your letter, we say to you as follows: It is not wisdom for you to go out of Caldwell with your families yet for a little season; until we are out of prison; after which you may act at your pleasure; but though you take your families out of the State, it will be necessary for you to return, and leave as before designed, on the 26th of April.

"Inasmuch as we are in prison, for a little season, if need be, the management of the affairs of the Church devolves on you, that is the Twelve.

"The gathering of necessity is stopped; but the conversion of the world need not stop, but under wise management can go on more rapidly than ever.

"Where churches are built, let them continue where they are, until a door is open to do otherwise, and let every Elder occupy his own ground, and when he builds a church, let him preside over it, and let not others run in to trouble him; and thus let every man prove himself unto God, that he is worthy. If we live, we live; and if we die for the testimony of Jesus, we die; but whether we live or die, let the work of God go on.

"Let the churches in England continue there till further orders—till a door can be opened for them, except they choose to come to America, and take their chance with the Saints here. If they will do that, let them come; and if they choose to come, they would do well to send their wise men before them, and buy out Kirtland, and the regions round about, or they may settle where they can till things may alter.

"It will be necessary for you to get the Twelve together, ordain such as have not been ordained, or at least such of them as you can get, and proceed to regulate the Elders as the Lord may give you wisdom. We nominate George A. Smith and Lyman Sherman to take the places of Orson Hyde and Thomas B. Marsh.

"Brethren, fear not, but be strong in the Lord and in the power of His might. What is man that the servant of God should fear him, or the son of man, that he should tremble at him. Neither think it strange concerning the fiery trials with which we are tried, as though some strange thing had happened unto us. Remember that all have been partakers of like afflictions. Therefore, rejoice in our afflictions, by which you are perfected and through which the Captain of our Salvation was perfected also. Let your hearts and the hearts of all the Saints be comforted with you, and let them rejoice exceedingly, for great is our reward in heaven, for so the wicked persecuted the prophets which were before us. America will be a Zion to all that choose to come to it; and if the churches in foreign countries wish to come, let them do so. Say to brother P. P. Pratt that our feelings accord with his; he is as we are, and we as he. May peace rest upon him in life and in death.

"Brethren, pray for us, and cease not till our deliverance comes, which we hope may come. We *hope*, we say, for our families' sake.

"Let the Elders preach nothing but the first principles of the gospel, and let them publish our afflictions—the injustice and cruelty thereof, upon the house tops. Let them write it and publish it in all the papers where they go. Charge them particularly on this point.

"Brethren we remain yours in hope of eternal life,

"SIDNEY RIGDON.

"JOSEPH SMITH JR.

"HYRUM SMITH.

"N. B. Appoint the oldest of those of the Twelve, who were first appointed, to be the president of your quorum.

"J. S.

"S. R.

"H. S."

On the 7th of February, 1839, I accompanied Brother Brigham to Liberty, to visit Joseph and the brethren in prison. We had the privilege of going in to see and converse with them. We stayed at Liberty over night, and the next morning we were permitted to visit the prisoners again, while they were at breakfast. We returned during the day to Far West.

When we left there, Lyman Sherman was somewhat unwell, and in a few days after our return he died. We did not notify him of his appointment.

I fitted up a small wagon, procured a span of ponies, and sent my wife and three children out of the State in company with Brother Brigham Young and his family, and several others, who left Far West February 14th. Everything my family took with them out of Missouri, could have been packed on the backs of two horses; the mob took all the rest.

Being a stranger in Missouri, I was requested by Joseph, Brigham and others to tarry and assist the committee in getting the brethren and families out of the State, and in waiting upon those brethren who were confined in prison.

On the 12th of March, I wrote to Joseph Fielding, Liverpool, England, saying: "I have only received two letters from you since I have come here. If you knew the feelings I have for the welfare of that people, your pen would not be so idle. May God stir you up to diligence to feed the sheep of God; for they are children of my begetting through the gospel. Think it not strange that I speak thus; for you know the feelings that a father has for his children.

"Now, brethren, be faithful and visit the churches, and exhort the Saints to be faithful in all things, and not lay down their watch for a moment; for there is great danger of falling beneath the powers of darkness. Don't think hard of me, brethren, for my plainness, for I am a plain man, and God requires it of me, and the same of you. Don't keep the Saints in ignorance of those things I have made you acquainted with—that is, our sufferings, for they will know them when I come, and they will have to pass through similar scenes. Don't be selfish; for it will not impoverish you to tell them all that I tell you.

"Your sister Mary left here about eight weeks ago, also the rest of the wives of the prisoners, thinking that they would be out in a few days. There are ten in prison; they are all well and in good spirits. I am going to see them to-morrow if the Lord will.

"Mobs are common in this country; it is getting so that there is no safety anywhere in this land. Prepare yourselves for trouble wherever you go, for it awaits you and all others that love the Lord and keep His commandments.

"Brethren, I want you to go to the north where Brother Russell labored, and see what situation the Saints are in, for I have some fears about them. Go and strengthen them in the name of the Lord. * * * * * *

"Brethren, I can truly say that I have never seen the Church in a better state since I have been a member of it. What there are left are firm and steadfast, full of love and good works. They have lost all their earthly goods, and are now ready to go and preach the gospel to a dying world. We have ordained about one hundred Elders into the Seventies. There are about one hundred and fifty who have gone into the vineyard this winter to preach the gospel, and many more will go in the spring, and several will come to England with me in the summer or fall. Elder Rigdon was bailed out of prison, and has left Missouri. About ten thousand had gathered to this State. By the 1st of May next there will not be one left who has any faith. Not one-fourth part had any teams to move with, and we had two hundred miles to travel before we could get out of the State. I think their deliverance is a great miracle."

About this time, Orson Hyde came to me, feeling very sorrowful for the course he had pursued the past few months. He said it was because of fear, and that he lamented his folly, and he asked me what he should do. I told him to give up his school, remove his family and gather with the Church. He wanted to know if I thought the brethren would forgive him. I said, "Yes."

He then asked, "Will you defend my case?" and I promised him I would.

On the 15th, the Prophet Joseph and others petitioned Judge Tompkins, or either of the supreme judges of the State of Missouri, for a States writ of *habeas corpus*, that he and his brethren might be brought before either of those judges, that justice might be administered. I was requested by Joseph to go to Jefferson and present the petition.

Theodore Turley accompanied me. We took copies of the papers by which the prisoners were held, with the petition to the supreme judges, and immediately started a distance of three hundred miles. We visited the judges, and laid the whole matter before them individually, according to our best ability. Neither of them would take any action in the case, although they appeared friendly and acknowledged that they were illegally imprisoned. We also presented a petition to the secretary of state, the governor being absent. He appeared very kind, but like the other officers, he *had no power to do good.*

We immediately returned to Liberty, where we arrived on the 3rd, and made Joseph and the prisoners acquainted with the result of our mission—through the gate of the dungeon, as we were not permitted to enter the prison.

Joseph told us to be of good cheer, for the Lord would deliver him and his brethren in due time. He also told us to advise the brethren to keep up their spirits, and get all the Saints away as fast as possible.

In company with Brother Turley, I visited Judge Austin A. King, who was vexed at us for presenting his illegal papers to the supreme judges. He treated us very roughly.

I returned to Far West April 5th, and remained a few days. My family having been gone about two months (during which time I heard nothing from them), our brethren being in prison, and death and destruction following us wherever we went, I felt very sorrowful and lonely. While in this condition, the following words came to my mind, and the Spirit said unto me, "write." I obeyed by taking a piece of paper and writing on my knee, as follows:

"FAR WEST,

"April 6, 1839.

"*A Word from the Spirit of the Lord to My Servant Heber C. Kimball:*

"Verily, I say unto my servant Heber, thou art my son in whom I am well pleased; for thou art careful to hearken to my words, and not transgress my law nor rebel against my servant Joseph Smith; for thou hast a respect to the words of mine anointed, even from the least to the greatest of them; therefore, thy name is written in heaven, no more to be blotted out forever, because of these things; and this spirit and blessing shall rest down upon thy posterity forever and ever; for they shall be called after thy name, for thou shalt have many more sons and daughters, for thy seed shall be as numerous as the sands upon the sea shore. Therefore, my servant Heber, be faithful; go forth in my name and I will go with you, and be on your right hand and on your left, and my angels shall go before you and raise you up when you are cast down and afflicted. Remember that I am always with you, even to the end; therefore, be of good cheer, my son, and my Spirit shall be in your heart, to teach you the peaceable things of the kingdom. Trouble not thyself about thy family, for they are in my hands; I will feed them and clothe them and make unto them friends. They never shall want for food nor raiment, houses nor lands, fathers nor mothers, brothers nor sisters; and peace shall rest upon them forever, if thou wilt be faithful and go forth and preach my gospel to the nations of the earth; for thou shalt be blessed in this thing. Thy tongue shall be loosed to such a degree that has not entered into thy heart as yet, and the children of men shall believe thy words, and flock to the water, even as they did to my servant John; for thou shalt be great in winning souls to me, for this is thy gift and calling. And there shall be no gift withheld from thee, if thou art faithful; therefore, be faithful, and I will give thee favor in the eyes of the people. Be humble and kind, and thou shalt obtain kindness; be merciful, and thou shalt obtain mercy; and I will be with thee even unto the end. Amen."

CHAPTER XIII

Judge King having ordered the removal of the prisoners from Liberty to Daviess County, fearing that we might get a change of venue to some other place, Brother Daniel Shearer and I were appointed to visit Judge Hughes, who had formerly been an Indian agent, and get him to go to Daviess and attend the sitting of the court there. He expressed himself in friendly terms towards Joseph and the brethren. Being a very rough man in his language, he cursed the judges and the governor and everybody else that would not step forward and help our friends out of the hands of their persecutors, for he did not believe they were guilty of any of the crimes alleged against them. Said he, "There is no proof that these men have committed any crime worthy of imprisonment or death, and the Mormons have been treated mean." Looking us directly in the eye, he said, with an oath, "Look at their eyes; see how bright and keen they are! They are whipped but not conquered; you can see that in their eyes."

There were several men in Liberty who were very friendly to the brethren. I called on them when I went there and they treated me with great civility. Among these were General Doniphan and Atchison and the keeper of the tavern where I put up at, and several of the foremost men who belonged to the masonic fraternity.

Those men whom I have named, and several others, revolted at the scenes enacted against the "Mormons," and would have liberated the brethren, had it not been for the "outside pressure," that is, the strong prejudices imbibed by the people generally against us, and their blood-thirsty desire to kill the Prophets.

I sent one hundred dollars by Brother Stephen Markham to Joseph, and also various sums at different times by other individuals.

The mob continued to threaten the few Saints who remained in Far West, and accordingly on the 14th of April, 1838, the committee, who had been left there to look after the wants of the poor, removed thirty-six of the helpless families into Tenney's grove, about twenty-five miles from Far West. I was obliged to secrete myself in the corn-fields and woods during the day and only venture out in the evening, to counsel the committee and brethren in private houses.

On the morning of the 18th, as I was going to the committee room to tell the brethren to wind up their affairs and be off, or their lives would be taken, I was met on the public square by several of the mob. One of them asked, with an oath, if I was a "Mormon."

I replied, "I am a 'Mormon.'"

With a series of blasphemous expressions, they then threatened to blow my brains out, and also tried to ride over me with their horses, in the presence of Elias Smith, Theodore Turley and others of the committee.

It was but a few minutes after I had notified the committee to leave before the mob gathered at the tithing house, and began breaking clocks, chairs, windows, looking-glasses and furniture, and making a complete wreck of everything they could move, while Captain Bogart, the County judge, looked on and laughed. A mobber named Whittaker threw an iron pot at the head of Theodore Turley and hurt him considerably, when Whittaker jumped about and laughed like a mad man; and all this at the time when we were using our utmost endeavors to get the Saints away from Far West. The brethren gathered up what they could, and fled from Far West in one hour. The mob staid until the committee left, and then plundered thousands of dollars worth of property which had been left by the brethren and sisters to assist the poor to remove.

One mobber rode up, and, finding no convenient place to fasten his horse to, shot a cow that was standing near, while a girl was milking her, and while the poor animal was struggling in death, he cut a strip of her hide from the nose to her tail, to which he fastened his halter.

During the commotion of this day, a great portion of the records of the committee, accounts, history, etc., were destroyed or stolen.

Hearing that Joseph and his brethren had escaped from their guard while they were on their way from Daviess to Boone County, to which place they had obtained a change of venue, I called on Shadrach Roundy, with whom I started immediately towards Quincy, Illinois.

On reaching Keetsville I stopped at the house of Colonel Price. The Colonel hearing of my arrival, came directly into the house, and, discovering who I was, said, "Joseph and Hyrum Smith and the other prisoners have escaped."

I enquired what he knew about them, and he answered, "Their guard took breakfast here this morning. They have turned back, saying they were going back to Richmond, by way of Tenney's grove. I know that the guards have been bribed, or they would evince more interest in pursuing them."

After we had partaken of refreshments, Brother Roundy and I pursued our course towards Quincy about fourteen or fifteen miles, when, being thoroughly satisfied that the prisoners had escaped, we turned back towards Far West.

When we arrived at Tenney's grove, a man came to me and presented an order drawn on me, by Joseph Smith, for five hundred dollars, saying it was for horses furnished him. I immediately raised four hundred dollars and paid him, when he proceeded to Richmond, Ray County, where he paid out the money to secure some of the lands that we had been driven from.

Brother Roundy and I started a few hours afterwards for Richmond, being on our way to Far West, for the purpose of visiting Parley P. Pratt and others in jail.

On our arrival at Richmond, I went directly to the prison to see Parley, but was prohibited by the guard, who said they would blow my brains out if I attempted to go near him. In a few minutes, Sister Morris Phelps came to me in great agitation and advised me to leave forthwith, as Brother Pratt had told her that a large body of men had assembled with tar, feathers and a rail, who swore they would tar and feather me, and ride me on the rail. They suspected I was the one who had assisted Joseph and the other prisoners to escape.

I immediately informed Brother Roundy, and we jumped on our horses and fled towards Far West, which was forty miles distant. We rode all night and reached Far West about the break of day. Expecting Brother Brigham Young and the Twelve to arrive there that day, I kept myself concealed in the woods, and passed around the country notifying the brethren and sisters to be on hand at the appointed time to witness the work upon the temple.

On the night of April 25th, which was pleasant, clear and moonlight, Elders Brigham Young, Orson Pratt, John E. Page, John Taylor, Wilford Woodruff, George A. Smith and Alphens Cutler arrived from Quincy, Illinois, and rode into the public square early on the morning of the 26th. All seemed still as death.

We held a conference at the house of Brother Samuel Clark, cut off thirty-one persons from the Church, and then proceeded to the building spot of the Lord's house, where, after singing a hymn on the mission of the Twelve, we recommenced laying the foundation, agreeable to the revelation given July 8th, 1838, by rolling a stone, upwards of a ton in weight, upon or near the south-east corner.

We ordained Wilford Woodruff and George A. Smith, who had been previously nominated by the First Presidency, accepted by the Twelve, and acknowledged by the Church at Quincy, members of the quorum of the Twelve Apostles. We ordained as Seventies, Darwin Chase and Norman Shearer, who had been liberated from Richmond prison two days previously, where they had been confined about six months for the cause of Christ.

The Twelve then, individually called upon the Lord in prayer in the following order: Brigham Young, Heber C. Kimball, Orson Pratt, John E. Page, John Taylor, Wilford Woodruff and George A. Smith, kneeling on the corner stone; after which "Adam-ondi-Ahman" was sung, when the Twelve took leave of the Saints, agreeable to the revelation.

The brethren wandered among our deserted houses, many of which were in ruins, and saw the streets in many places grown over with grass.

We went to Father Clark's, got breakfast, and before sunrise we departed. We rode thirty miles that day, and camped at night with the families of Elders Clark and Turley.

On arriving at Quincy on the 2nd of May, I found my family well and in good spirits; and on reading the words of inspiration which I had written, my wife bore record to the truth of that part which says, "Trouble not thyself about thy family, for they are in my hands. I will feed them and clothe them and make unto them friends," etc. I learned from her that my family continued with Brother Brigham until they crossed the Mississippi to the town of Atlas, in Illinois, where, through the instrumentality of George Pitkin, my wife got introduced to a Widow Ross, who let her have a comfortably-fitted-up room, and the privilege of cooking by her fire, and who was as kind to her as an own mother or sister. Here my wife tarried seven weeks, and only had to pay fifty cents a week. At the end of that time, John P. Greene came with his wagon and horses and carried my family up to Quincy, forty miles, and rented a good room where I found her.

She had had no lack of friends and had every comfort bestowed upon her that she could have had among her own kindred; and I can say in my heart, God bless all who aided and assisted my family. Jesus says every man shall be rewarded for every good deed that he doeth and even if a man giveth a cup of cold water to a disciple he shall receive a disciple's reward.

In relation to that part of the Lord's word to me which said I should have many sons and daughters, my wife was rather in doubt, as she considered she was too advanced in years, and the thought had never entered our minds that the Lord would establish in this Church the doctrine of plurality of wives in my day; still I believed it would be restored to the earth in some future time.

CHAPTER XIV

JOYFUL MEETING WITH JOSEPH—FIRST CONFERENCE
IN ILLINOIS—FIRST VISIT TO COMMERCE—MY IMPRESSION
CONCERNING THE NEW GATHERING PLACE—MY RECOMMEND—
STRUGGLE WITH EVIL SPIRITS—JOSEPH SMITH'S EXPERIENCE
WITH EVIL SPIRITS—P. P. PRATT'S ESCAPE FROM PRISON—
BUILDING HOUSES—PROSTRATED WITH SICKNESS—
REMARKABLE MANIFESTATION OF THE GIFT OF HEALING.

On the 3rd of May, 1839, in company with Elders Brigham Young, O. Pratt, John Taylor, W. Woodruff and George A. Smith, I rode four miles to Mr. Cleaveland's, to visit Joseph and Hyrum, who were as glad to see us as we were to see them once more enjoying their liberty. I spent the day with them and it was one of the greatest days of rejoicing in my life to once more have the privilege of conversing with the Prophet in freedom.

The next day I attended a general conference of the Church near Quincy, at which the Saints from all the regions round about assembled. It was a time which will long be remembered by the Saints, being the first conference held after their expulsion.

The cases of Brothers William Smith and Orson Hyde were brought up. I had previously informed Brother Hyrum Smith of Orson Hyde's feelings of repentance, and desire to return to the Church. Hyrum partook of the spirit, and when Joseph presented the name of Orson Hyde before the Church, Hyrum and I plead for him according to the spirit that was in us. Joseph then remarked, "If my brother Hyrum and Heber C. Kimball will defend Orson Hyde, I will withdraw my motion."

The conference granted them the privilege of appearing personally before the next conference of the Church, to give an account of their conduct, but required that in the meantime they both be suspended from executing the functions of their office.

The conference sanctioned the proceeding of the Twelve on the temple block at Far West, on the 26th of April, and also the intended mission of the Twelve to Europe.

The conference continued for three days, and a most agreeable time was enjoyed. Elder Rigdon was appointed delegate to go to Washington and lay the grievances of the Saints before the general government, and it was also resolved that a number of Elders should accompany the Twelve on their mission to Europe.

On Sunday, the 12th of May, I went up to Commerce, in company with some of the Twelve, in a wagon.

On the 25th I crossed the river with several of my brethren and spent the day in council with Joseph and others. While crossing the Mississippi, I was standing by the railing of the boat, looking at the beautiful site of Nauvoo, and remarked, "It is a very pretty place, but not a long abiding place for the Saints."

These remarks reached the ears of Elder Rigdon and family, and caused them to feel somewhat sad, as they were well situated in a nice stone house. When we met in council, in the house of Joseph Smith, Elder Rigdon said he had some feelings toward Elder Kimball, and added, "I should suppose that Elder Kimball had passed through sufferings and privations and mobbings and drivings enough to learn to prophesy good concerning Israel."

I saw that I was likely to receive quite a chastisement from Elder Rigdon, and knowing his peculiar temperament, I arose and said, "President Rigdon, I'll prophesy good concerning you all the time if you can get it!"

On hearing that, Joseph had a hearty laugh with the brethren, and Elder Rigdon yielded the point.

I here insert a recommend from the Presidency:

"To the Saints Scattered Abroad, to the Nations of Europe and to the World:

"Be it known unto you that Heber C. Kimball is fully authorized to preach the gospel of Jesus Christ, and his testimony can be relied on. He is a man of unexceptionable character, and received his authority and Priesthood from under the hands of the presiding authorities of the Church of Jesus Christ of Latter-day Saints, who were called by actual revelation from God. Therefore, God will bless him, and bear record by His power, thereby confirming his word and ministry. Thus testifieth your humble servants,

"SIDNEY RIGDON,

"HYRUM SMITH,

"JOSEPH SMITH, JR.

"QUINCY, ILL., June 3, 1839."

I wrote to P. P. Pratt, giving him the particulars of our conference at Far West on the 26th of April, and the resolution that the Twelve should have their shackles taken off, that they might go forth into the world to preach the gospel, and that the Bishops were to provide for our families, etc. I also added, "The Presidency feel well towards you. They say you must come out of that place, and so I say; for I do not feel as though I can go to England until I take you by the hand. When this takes place my joy will be full. Be of good cheer, brother; a few days now, and you shall see the salvation of God; and I shall see you in other lands, publishing peace to the captives. My determination is to be a man of God, and to try to save souls from their sins, let others do as they may. I will try to keep my eye on the mark, that is, Christ, the Son of the living God, His grace assisting me. The Twelve have all left Quincy. Orson is about twenty-five miles from here. Whatever you do, do quickly!"

Joseph advised those of the Twelve whose families were not at Commerce to remove them immediately to the new gathering place. I accordingly went to Quincy and removed my family up to a place belonging to Brother Bozier, about one mile from Commerce, where I pulled down an old stable and laid up the logs at the back end of the Bozier house, putting a few shakes on to cover it; but it had no floor or chinking. In this condition I moved my family into it. Whenever it rained the water stood nearly ankle deep on the ground in the house. There were some half-a-dozen families in the Bozier house.

The 25th, 26th and 27th of June I spent in council with the Presidency and Twelve, and received much valuable instruction from the Prophet. At this conference Orson Hyde appeared, made a humble confession, and was restored to the Priesthood.

One night I was awakened out of my sleep by my wife making a noise as though she was nearly choking to death. I inquired the cause, and she replied that she had dreamed that a personage came and seized her by the throat and was choking her. I immediately lit a candle and saw that her eyes were sunken and her nose pinched in as though she was in the last stage of the cholera. I laid hands upon her and rebuked the evil spirit in the name of Jesus, and by the power of the holy Priesthood commanded it to depart. In a moment afterwards I heard some half a dozen children in different parts of the Bozier house crying as if in great distress. The cattle also began to bellow, the horses neighed, the dogs barked, the hogs squealed, the hens cackled and roosters crowed, and everything around seemed in great commotion. In a few minutes afterwards I was sent for to lay hands upon Sister Patten, the widow of David W. Patten, who was living in the room adjoining mine, and who was seized in a similar manner to my wife.

My wife continued quite feeble for several days from the shock.

One day while visiting Joseph, he took me for a walk by the river side, when he requested me to relate the occurrence at Brother Bozier's. After I had done so, I also told him the vision of evil spirits in England, on the opening of the gospel to that people. After I had done this, I asked him what all these things meant, and whether or not there was anything wrong in me. He said:

"No, Brother Heber; at that time, when you were in England, you were nigh unto the Lord, there was only a veil between you and Him, but you could not see Him. When I heard of it, it gave me great joy; for I then knew that the work of God had taken root in that land. It was this that caused the devil to make a struggle to kill you."

Joseph then said the nearer a person approached to the Lord, the greater power would be manifest by the devil to prevent the accomplishment of the purposes of God.

He also gave me a relation of many contests that he had had with Satan, and his power that had been manifested from time to time since the commencement of bringing forth the Book of Mormon.

I will relate one circumstance that took place in Far West, in a house which Joseph had purchased, which had been formerly occupied as a public house by some wicked people. A short time after he had moved into it, one of the children was taken very sick. He laid his hands upon the child, when it got better. As soon as he went outside, the child was taken sick again. He again laid his hands upon it, so that it again recovered. This transpired several times, and Joseph inquired of the Lord what it all meant, when he had an open vision, and saw the devil in person, who contended with Joseph face to face for some time. He said it was his house, it belonged to him, and Joseph had no right there. Then Joseph rebuked Satan in the name of the Lord, and he departed and troubled the child no more.

On the 2nd of July, I went with Joseph, Hyrum, Sidney and others over the river to Montrose, after which we rode four miles and looked at the site for the town of Zarahemla. We dined at Brother Woodruff's. After dinner we all went to President Brigham Young's, where Brothers Woodruff and George A. Smith were blessed as two of the Twelve Apostles. Brother Hyrum Smith gave the Twelve some good advice on the nature of their mission — to practice prudence and humility in their preaching, and to strictly hold on to the authority of the Priesthood. Brother Joseph taught many glorious things and important principles to benefit and bless them on their mission; advising them to observe charity, wisdom and a fellow feeling for each other under all circumstances. He also unfolded the keys of knowledge, to detect Satan, and preserve us in the favor of God.

On Sunday, the 7th of July, I was present at a large meeting of the Saints in the open air to listen to the farewell addresses of the Twelve. Many were present who did not belong to the Church. After the meeting was dismissed three persons went forward and were baptized and confirmed.

On the 10th of July, Elder P. P. Pratt returned from his imprisonment in Missouri. When I heard that he was in Quincy I went there and assisted him and his brother Orson up to Commerce. His escape caused much rejoicing among the Saints.

In a few days afterwards he and I purchased from Hyrum Kimball five acres each of woodland, situated one mile from the river, and went to work to cut each a set of logs to build a house 14 by 16 feet, which we cut in one day. We then invited some of the old citizens, such as Brother Bozier, 'Squire Wells, Louis Robinson and others, to come and assist us to put them up, as our people were mostly prostrate with sickness. I got a man to assist me to hew puncheons for the floor, and to make some shakes, that is, strips of timber similar to barrel staves, with which to cover the roof. I also drew the rock and built a chimney, and just got it built to the ridge of the house, when I was stricken down with the chills and fever. My wife was also laid prostrate with the same.

A great amount of sickness prevailed among the inhabitants of Commerce, in consequence of the sufferings and hardships to which they had been subjected in being driven from Missouri; so that the time of those who were able to be about was generally spent in administering to the sick. Some had faith and were healed; to those who had not faith we administered mild herbs and nursed them as well as possible under the circumstances; but many died.

On the morning of the 22nd, the Prophet Joseph Smith arose from his bed of sickness, when the power of God rested upon him, and he went forth administering to the sick. He commenced with the sick in his own house, then visited those who were tenting in his door-yard, commanding the sick in the name of the Lord Jesus Christ to arise from their beds and be made whole, and they were healed according to his words. He then went from house to house and from tent to tent, on the bank of the river, healing the sick by the power of Israel's God as he went among them. He did not miss a single house, wagon or tent, and continued this work up to the "Upper Stone House," where he crossed the river, accompanied by P. P. Pratt, O. Pratt, John Taylor, John E. Page and myself, and walked into the cabin of Brother Brigham Young, who was lying very sick, and commanded him in the name of the Lord Jesus to arise and be made whole. He arose, healed of his sickness, and accompanied Joseph and his brethren of the Twelve. They went into the house of Brother Elijah Fordham, who was insensible and considered by his family and friends to be dying. Joseph stepped to his bedside, looked him in the eye for a minute without speaking, then took him by the hand and commanded him in the name of Jesus Christ to arise from his bed and walk. Brother Fordham instantly leaped out of his bed, threw off all his poultices and bandages, dressed himself, called for a bowl of bread and milk, which he ate, and then followed us into the street.

We then went into the house of Joseph B. Noble, who was also very sick, and he was healed in the same manner.

Joseph spoke with the voice and power of God.

When he had healed all the sick by the power given unto him, he went down to the ferry boat, when a stranger rode up almost breathless and said he had heard that "Jo" Smith was raising the dead and healing all the sick, and his wife begged of him to ride up and get Mr. Smith to go down and heal his twin children, who were about five months old. Joseph replied, "I cannot go, but will send some one." In a few minutes he said to Elder Woodruff, who lived in Montrose, "You go and heal those children. Take this pocket handkerchief, and when you administer to them, wipe their faces with it, and they shall recover." Brother Woodruff did as he was commanded, and the children were healed.

The mob leaders when they saw men, whom they thought were dying, arise from their beds and pray for others, stood paralyzed with fear, yet those same men would have killed Joseph and his brethren if they had had an opportunity.

Joseph recrossed the river and returned to his own house, and I went to my home, rejoicing in the mercies and goodness of God.

This was a day never to be forgotten by the Saints, nor by the wicked, for they saw the power of God manifest in the flesh.

CHAPTER XV

START UPON A MISSION UNDER DISTRESSING
CIRCUMSTANCES — INCIDENTS OF THE JOURNEY — A
DRUNKEN DOCTOR GIVES ME A TABLE-SPOONFUL OF
MORPHINE — MY LIFE SAVED THROUGH THE PRAYER OF
FAITH — BRETHREN LEAVE ME TO PROCEED TO KIRTLAND —
THEIR FEAR THAT I WOULD DIE — I PREDICT THAT I WOULD
RECOVER AND REACH KIRTLAND BEFORE THEM.

On the 4th of August, the Saints met to partake of the sacrament, and received an exhortation from the Prophet, impressing upon them the necessity of being righteous and clean of heart before the Lord, and commanding the Twelve to go forth without purse or scrip; according to the revelations of Jesus Christ.

My son David Patten was born during the night of the 23d in the log cabin which I had put up at the end of the Bozier house, and during the night we had a heavy thunder storm, but the hand of the Lord was over us.

As soon as my wife was able, I moved my family into the log house that I had built. Being without a house, Brother Orson Pratt moved his family in with mine.

On the 4th of September, President Brigham Young left his home at Montrose to start upon his mission to England. He was so sick that he was unable to go to the river, a distance of thirty rods, without assistance. After he had crossed the river, he rode behind Israel Barlow on his horse to my house, where he continued sick until the 18th. He left his wife sick with a babe only ten days old, and all his other children were sick and unable to wait upon one another. Not one of them was able to go to the well for a pail of water, and they were without a single change of clothes, for the mob in Missouri had taken nearly all he had.

On the 17th, Sister Mary Ann Young got a boy to carry her up in his wagon to my house, that she might nurse and comfort Brother Brigham to the hour of starting.

On the 18th, Charles Hubbard sent a boy with a wagon and span of horses to my house to start us on our journey. Our trunks were put into the wagon by some of the brethren who had come to bid us farewell.

I went to my bed and shook hands with my wife, who was then shaking with the ague, and had two of our children lying sick by her side. I embraced her and my children, and bade them farewell. The only child well was little Heber Parley, and it was with difficulty that he could carry a couple of quarts of water at a time, to assist in quenching their thirst.

With some difficulty we got into the wagon and started down the hill about ten rods. It seemed to me as though my very inmost parts would melt within me at the thought of leaving my family in such a condition, as it were almost in the arms of death. I felt as though I could scarcely endure it. I said to the teamster "hold up!" then turning to Brother Brigham I added, "This is pretty tough, but let's rise, and give them a cheer." We arose, and swinging our hats three times over our heads, we cried, "Hurrah, hurrah, hurrah for Israel!"

My wife, hearing the noise, arose from her bed and came to the door to see what was up. She had a smile on her face. She and Sister Young then cried out to us, "Good bye; God bless you!" We returned the compliment, and were pleased to see that they were so cheerful. We then told the driver to go ahead.

After this I felt a spirit of joy and gratitude at having the satisfaction of seeing my wife standing upon her feet, instead of leaving her in bed, knowing well that I should not see her again for two or three years.

We were without purse or scrip, and were carried across the prairie, about fourteen miles, to a shanty near the railway, where Brother O. M. Duell lived.

On arriving there, we were unable to carry our small trunks into the house, and Sister Duell, seeing our feeble condition, assisted the boy to carry them in. We were very much fatigued, and as soon as we got into the house Sister Duell made us a cup of tea; which revived us, and prepared a bed for us on a one-legged bedstead in a corner of the house, having two poles running from the house logs to the leg.

In the course of the night our bedstead broke through, and we found ourselves on the floor, between the poles and the side of the house.

The following day Brother Duell took us in his wagon to Lima, about twelve miles, when he left us. He gave each of us a dollar to assist us on our journey. Brother Bidwell then carried us in his wagon to John A. Mikesell's, near Quincy, about twenty miles.

The fatigue of this day's journey was too much for our feeble health; we were prostrated, and obliged to tarry a few days in Quincy to recruit.

The brethren preached a few times in a meeting house close to the Congregational church. The members of the latter church were in the habit of commencing their meetings at different hours from the brethren, but they took a notion to disturb us, by ringing their bell furiously after we had commenced our meetings. At one time Elder John E. Page preached so loud as to drown the noise of the bell, and this brought some hundreds, who otherwise would not have come, to meeting.

I was prostrate with the chills and fever, and stayed most of the time at the house of Sisters Laura and Abigail Pitkin, who bestowed every kindness upon me they possibly could. Dr. Orlando Hovey, and Sister Staley and her daughter were also very kind in administering to me in my feeble condition.

We left Quincy September 25th, feeling much better. My sorrow was great to see so many of our brethren there sick and dying, in consequence of being driven and exposed to hunger and cold.

Brother Lyman Wight took us in a one-horse wagon to Brother Charles C. Rich's, at Burton; where we stayed through the night. Brother Wight predicted many good things, and left this blessing with us, when he bade us farewell.

The following day while Brother Rich was taking us to Brother Wilbur's, the chills came on me again, and I suffered much pain and fatigue.

On the 27th, Brother Wilbur took us in a buggy about twenty-five miles to the house of James Allred, in Pittsfield, and the following day Father Allred conveyed us to the place where Brother Harlow Redfield lived, where we preached to a small branch of the Church on Sunday, the 29th.

On the 30th, Brother Rodgers carried Brother Brigham to Brother Decker's, and me to the house of Mr. Roswell Murray, my father-in-law. They were living within a few rods of each other, near Winchester, in Scott County.

Here we also found a few brethren in the Church, who had been smitten and robbed of their property in Missouri, but were once more in comfortable circumstances and rejoicing in the Lord.

On the 1st of October, we were conveyed to Lorenzo D. Young's, where we remained and recruited our strength until the 4th, when he conveyed us to Jacksonville.

On the 5th, a sister in the Church hired a horse and buggy to take us to Springfield, a distance of thirty-five miles, and Brother Babcock drove for us. There we were kindly received by brethren, and nursed. Brother

Brigham being confined to his bed by sickness, Brother Libeus T. Coon, who was practicing medicine, waited upon him. Here we found Brothers G. A. Smith, T. Turley and R. Hedlock.

I went from house to house strengthening and comforting the brethren, and teaching them the things of the kingdom. I was so far recovered that I preached on the Sabbath, which caused a great feeling of love towards us. The Saints got a two horse wagon and harness for us, for which they paid fifty-five dollars, and also collected thirty-five dollars in money for the company. Judge Adams, of the supreme court, took me to his house. I stayed with him three nights and the greater part of three days, and he gave me five dollars when I left.

While we remained at Springfield, the sisters fitted up a bed in the wagon for Brother Brigham to ride on, as he was unable to sit up.

On the 11th of October, I resumed my journey, in company with Brothers Young, Turley, Smith and Hedlock.

We traveled eight miles and put up at the house of Father Draper. When we went into the house, Brother George A. Smith, while stooping down to warm at the fire, dropped a small flask bottle, containing tonic bitters, out of his pocket on the hearth, and broke it. At this occurrence, Father Draper was very much astonished, and said, "You are a pretty set of Apostles, to be carrying a bottle of whisky with you!"

We explained to him that the bottle contained some bitters which the brethren at Springfield had prepared for Brother George A., because of his sickness. This appeased his righteous soul, so that he consented to allow us to stay through the night.

On the following day, we pursued our journey towards Terre Haute, most of the brethren being very sick. Owing to the bad roads, I walked most of the way. At might I slept in a wagon and caught cold. The next morning I had to go till twelve o'clock before I had anything to eat, and then it was transparent pork and corn dodger. My health again began to fail. The wagon broke down twice and the chills came on me about two in the afternoon and held me till night, then the fever held me all night. I had the chills and fever three days, and lost my appetite. The third chill was so severe that it seemed as though I could not live till night.

We arrived at Terre Haute about dusk on the 17th. Brother Young and I put up at Dr. Modisett's, and the other brethren and Father Murray, my father-in-law, who had accompanied us on a visit to his friends in the east, stayed at Milton Stowe's, who lived in one of the doctor's houses. In the evening the doctor went to see them, as they were quite ill, and Brother Stowe was very poor. The doctor expressed great sympathy for them when he returned to his house, * * seeing them in ill health and lying on a straw bed on the floor. He shed many tears at thoughts of the brethren going under such suffering circumstances upon such a long mission; but he did not have quite sympathy enough to buy them a chicken to make them some broth, or even give them a shilling, although he was worth four or five hundred thousand dollars. He said his taxes amounted to over four hundred dollars a year.

In the evening I became very ill. The doctor said he could give me something that would do me good and relieve me of my distress, and I would probably get a nap; but the old man was so drunk that he did not know what he did, and he gave me a table-spoonfull of morphine. His wife saw him pour it out; but dared not say a word, although she believed it would kill me.

In a few minutes after I took it, I straightened up in my chair, complaining of feeling very strangely, and as though I wanted to lie down. On my attempting to go to the bed, I reeled and fell to the floor. There was hardly a breath of life in my body. Brother Brigham rolled me over on my back, put a pillow under my head and inquired of the doctor what he had given me, and then learned that he had given me morphine. I lay there for a long time; when I came to, Brother Brigham was attending to me with a fatherly care, and manifesting much anxiety in my behalf. I remarked, "Don't be scared; for I shan't die."

In a short time after, he got me on the bed, and nursed me through the night. I commenced vomiting and continued doing so most of the night. He changed my under-clothes five times, and washed me each time previous to changing, as I was covered with a cold sweat. It was through the closest attention of Brother Young and the family that my life was preserved through the night. I was scarcely able to speak so as to be understood.

In the morning, Brothers Smith, Turley, Hedlock and Father Murray came to see us, and the brethren laid their hands upon me and prayed for me. When they left they wept like children. Father Murray felt very sorrowful. Said he, "We shall never see Heber again; he will die." I looked up at them and said, "Never mind, brethren; go ahead, for Brother Brigham and I will reach Kirtland before you will." Brother Brigham gave them all the money we had except five dollars, and told them to take good care of the team and make all possible speed to Kirtland. They started the same day. In about an hour after their departure I arose from my bed.

CHAPTER XVI

FURTHER INCIDENTS OF THE JOURNEY—MONEY
INCREASED BY THE POWER OF GOD—ARRIVE AT
KIRTLAND AHEAD OF BRETHREN, IN FULFILLMENT OF MY
PREDICTION—SERVICES IN THE TEMPLE—VISIT MY OLD
HOME AND MY RELATIVES—KIND TREATMENT—ARRIVE
IN NEW YORK—JOYFUL MEETING WITH BRETHREN.

On the 22nd of October, Elder Almon W. Babbitt and Dr. Knight, an eminent physician, came from Pleasant Garden to see me, and the next day Brother James Modisett took us in his father's carriage twenty miles, to the house of Brother Addison Pratt. From there we were conveyed by Dr. Knight to Pleasant Garden, and put up with Brother Jonathan Crosby. We found a few brethren there, who were well and in good spirits. We remained three days, preaching to the few brethren and those who wished to hear. * * *

Before leaving, Dr. Knight and some others gave us some money to assist us on our mission. While there I also received a letter from my wife, giving an account of her sickness since I left, also that of our children, William and Helen. I wrote her a comforting letter in reply, praying the Lord to bless her and the little ones.

On the 26th, Brother Babbitt took us in his buggy twelve miles, to the house of Brother Scott, whose family was very glad to see us, and we tarried with them through the night, after which Brother Scott sent his little son, John, to convey us to Bellville, fifteen miles, several miles of the journey in a rain storm, which obliged us to put up at an inn for the remainder of the day and night. Brother Brigham was very sick, and had to go to bed. I sat up to wait upon him, and spent the evening with the landlord and his lady, preaching to them. They received our testimony, and were very kind to us.

The following morning the landlord arose very early, and talked to the citizens about the travelers who had stayed with him the night previous, and what he had heard us say concerning the gospel. The neighbors flocked in; made many enquiries and were very anxious that we should tarry and preach in the place.

Our host said several times he hoped the stage would not come, that we might stay and preach, as the people were very much excited on account of a great discussion which had recently occurred between two popular preachers.

The stage, however, came along about ten o'clock, and we started on our way towards Kirtland, leaving the landlord in tears.

The money given to us in Pleasant Garden added to the five dollars we had left when the brethren parted from us on the 18th, amounted to thirteen dollars and fifty cents. When we got into the stage we did not expect to ride many miles. We rode, however, as far as Indianapolis, paid our passage, and found we had sufficient means to carry us to Richmond, Indiana. When we arrived in Richmond, we found we had means to take us to Dayton, to which place we proceeded and tarried over night, waiting for another line of stages. We expected to stop here and preach until we got means to pursue our journey. Brother Brigham, however, went to his trunk to get money to pay the bill and found we had sufficient to pay our passage to Columbus, to which place we took passage in the stage and tarried over night. When he paid the next bill, he found he had sufficient means to pay our passage to Worcester, and accordingly we took passage for that place. When we arrived there, Brother Brigham went to his trunk again to get money to pay, and found sufficient to pay our passage to Cleveland.

While on our way to Cleveland, and within about twenty miles of that place we passed a little town called Strongsville. Brother Brigham had a strong impression to stop at a tavern when we first came into that town; but as the stage did not stop there we went on.

We arrived at Cleveland about eleven o'clock at night, took lodgings and remained till next morning.

On the morning of November 3rd, it being Sunday, we went to the Episcopalian church, and while returning to the hotel, we met my father-in-law, and learned that Elders Smith, Turley and Hedlock had just arrived in Cleveland. Father Murray was as much astonished to see me alive as though he had seen one risen from the dead. I don't think I ever saw a man feel better than he did when I met him in the street.

We walked with him a short distance and met the brethren, whose health was good compared with what it had been, and who were in fine spirits. We learned that they had stayed over night at the tavern in Strongsville, where Brother Brigham had such a strong impression to stop the night previous. They had picked up Elder John Taylor at Dayton, where he was left at a tavern very sick with the ague a few days before, by Father Coltrin, who proceeded to Kirtland.

Brothers Taylor and Hedlock got into the stage with us, which left early in the afternoon, and rode as far as Willoughby. We proceeded to Kirtland and arrived the same evening, where we found a good many brethren and friends, who were glad to see us. Thus was the prediction fulfilled which I made on my sick bed, in regard to reaching Kirtland before my brethren.

Brother Brigham had one York shilling left, and on looking over our expenses, we found we had paid out over eighty-seven dollars out of the thirteen dollars and fifty cents we had at Pleasant Garden, which was all the money we had to pay our passage with. We had traveled over four hundred miles by stage, for which we paid from eight to ten cents a mile, and had taken three meals a day, for each of which we were charged fifty cents, also fifty cents for our lodgings. Brother Brigham often suspected that I put the money in his trunk or clothes, thinking that I had a purse of money which I had not acquainted him with; but this was not so; the money could only have been put in his trunk by some heavenly messenger, who thus administered to our necessities daily as he knew we needed.

There was a division of sentiment among the brethren in Kirtland, many of whom lacked the energy to move to Missouri, and some lacked the disposition.

On Sunday, the 10th of November, Elder John Taylor preached in the temple in the forenoon, and I preached in the afternoon. I had great freedom in speaking, and compared my hearers to a parcel of old earthen pots that were cracked in burning, for they were mostly apostates who were living there.

Immediately after I returned to the house of Ira Bond, Martin Harris, Cyrus Smalling and others came in and attacked me on what I had been saying, asking me who I referred to in my comparisons. I answered, "To no one in particular, but to anyone that the coat fits." I was so sick that I referred them to Brother Hedlock, who came in at that moment, to talk with, as I was lying on a bed, having a chill, and not able to talk. John Moreton and others declared I should never preach in the house again. Some of the people tried to make me angry, so as to quarrel with me, but they failed.

I made my home at Dean Gould's, in the house of Ira Bond. They were all very kind to me. I staid with them most of the time I was in Kirtland, during which the weather was very stormy.

I was thankful to get rid of the chills that time without the aid of medicine, but I continued afflicted with a cough which I caught by riding in the stage at night.

On Sunday, the 17th, Brother Brigham preached in the forenoon, and Brother John Taylor in the afternoon. In the evening Brother Brigham anointed Brother John Taylor in the house of the Lord, he having previously washed himself in pure water; then we all went to the temple. I was called upon and opened the meeting by prayer, when Brigham anointed him with pure sweet oil and pronounced such blessings upon him as the Spirit gave utterance to, and Brother Taylor then arose and prayed.

Brother Theodore Turley, one of the Seventies, was then anointed by Daniel S. Miles one of the presidents of the Seventies; both of which anointings were sealed by loud shouts of hosannah. Then their feet were washed and the meeting closed.

A council was held with Brothers Kellog, Moreton and others, who took the lead in Kirtland. We proposed that some of the Elders should remain there and preach for a few weeks, but John Moreton replied that they had had many talented preachers, and he considered that men of such ordinary ability as the missionaries of our party possessed could do no good in Kirtland; he thought possibly that Brother John Taylor *might* do, but he was not sure.

Kirtland at that time was a desolate looking place, about one-half of the houses being empty and going to ruin.

We had but little means to prosecute our journey, but, God being our helper, we felt to press our way onward.

I left there with my brethren on the 22nd of November, and went to Fairport. There we were detained till the 26th on account of a tremendous snow storm. Our board cost us fifteen dollars while there. We boarded a boat and landed at Buffalo on the 27th, in the morning, and proceeded by stage to Batavia, where we arrived in the evening. The next afternoon, we took the cars for Rochester.

When we got to Byron, I got out and left the brethren, supposing Harvy Hall, my brother-in-law, was living there. I had scarcely left the cars when I was informed that he had gone to Rochester. I think I never felt worse in my life, my anticipations were so great to see him, and I could not get away till the next night. Just at evening, I got aboard the cars and arrived at Hall's at eight the next evening, where I was joyfully received. I staid there one week, and was confined to my bed some of the time. I had to take deck passage on the steamboat for the want of means, and took cold and it settled in my right side. I was so bad that I could hardly draw my breath.

A letter from my wife reached Mendon, my old home about three weeks before I did. Sister Hall was at my brother Solomon's, and advised him to take it out. He did so, and opened it, but could not tell where I was. Supposing that I was dead, my relatives were feeling very badly when I arrived there. I was taken to my brother Solomon's, and he and his family were all rejoiced to see me once more in the land of the living.

Nathaniel Campbell, my wife's brother-in-law, came and took me home with him to Victor. I received great kindness from them and from all my old friends. Several of the neighbors came in while I was there, and my wife's sister introduced me as her "Mormon" brother. They seemed to take a great interest in our sufferings, and this seemed to be the feeling of all candid people.

I was urged by my friends to return and bring my family, and remain with them, or at least to stop there till warm weather, on account of my poor health, as a little fatigue would bring me down again. However, I knew it would not do, as "no man, having put his hand to the plow, and looking back, is fit for the kingdom of God."

I preached in Mendon school house Sunday, December 21st, at one o'clock. The house was full. Then in the evening again there was an appointment for their Methodist preacher, but as he did not come, nothing would do but I must preach. I also preached at Miller's Corner. There seemed to be a great desire to hear, but my health would not permit me to speak much.

On the 29th, Brother William E. Murray came through the snow up to his horses' sides, determined to have me go home with him. It was as much as we could do to get to his house. It was a pleasure to me to see them. William said to me, "When you want to pray, Heber, use your liberty." He and his family seemed to take much pleasure in the things of God; and on the first day of the year 1840, I went into the water and baptized him and his wife. He gave me a little money, a pair of pantaloons and a pair of drawers, and would have given me fifty dollars if he had had it. My sister, Mrs. Wheeler, gave me another pair of drawers and two fine shirts, and a shawl to wear around my neck. An old friend, John E. Tomlinson, gave me a dollar and said if I would come again he'd give me more. These, with Brother Wheeler, were the only ones who would help me upon my mission. Others were willing to assist me if I would only forsake my "Mormonism" and come back and live with them; but I felt that I would rather live in a cave, or be driven with the Saints every other year while I lived, and be one with them, than to apostatize and have all the good things of the earth, for I would feel myself disgraced in the sight of God and man.

On the 6th of January, I preached in Mendon for the fourth time. I also had calls to preach in other parts of the town, as well as other towns in that region. The Baptist church that I had formerly been a member of, had about died out.

While in Victor, I had several calls to go to Pike. After being much wrought upon, I consented to go. William Murray and wife accompanied me. We got to the house of my old friend, Adolphus Huit, the first day of February. I never saw a person more pleased than his wife was to see me; she said that she had been calling on the Lord that He would send me there.

On Sunday morning we went to the Christian chapel. After the meeting was through, an appointment was given out for me to preach on Monday evening. The church leaders said they were willing that I should preach, because the people were in such a cold state that I could not have any effect upon them.

When the time came, I went and found the house crowded. My text was from the 2nd Epistle of John, 9th, 10th and 11th verses. When I was almost through, two of the ministers came into the pulpit. I gave them permission to speak, when one Baptist arose and found fault with me because I had preached from the Bible.

When he had sat down, I answered him, and then three others followed his example, and I answered each in turn. They were confounded, and the discussion tended to open the eyes of the people.

I afterwards baptized Mrs. Huit, and many others believed. I only preached once and then returned to Victor.

On the 10th, I started for New York, and reached Albany on the 12th. Mr. Wheeler, my brother-in-law, stayed with me all night at the hotel and paid my bill. He thought me unwise to go any farther, but the next day I took coach for New York.

I went up on the east side of the river, crossed the Catskill Mountains, and took three days to get to Jersey City, traveling part of the way by sleigh. When I arrived at Jersey City, I had not one penny left, and could not cross the river without paying twenty-five cents. I informed the person in charge of the boat that I was out of money, and a gentleman who overheard me gave me twenty-five cents. I crossed the river into New York at nine o'clock at night, went to the Western Hotel and pawned my trunk to pay for lodging. I had only eaten one meal a day while traveling to New York, for want of money to buy more, but I did not suffer from hunger.

The next morning, I went in search of some of the Saints, and soon found Brothers Parley P. and Orson Pratt and Brigham Young, who were glad to see me. I went to meeting with them and found one hundred and fifty Saints assembled. It was a great pleasure to meet with them. They were very kind to me, and soon provided me with money to redeem my trunk.

I found a letter in New York from my wife, which had lain in the office for a long time, and I was thankful to hear that she and our children were better.

Soon after I arrived in New York, Orson Pratt and I were called upon to visit a sick woman, who was unable to turn herself in bed without assistance. We anointed her with oil in the name of the Lord, and she was made whole. She did not belong to the Church, nor did her husband, but in two days afterwards she and her husband were baptized, and fourteen others.

I was detained in New York about four weeks, being unable to obtain passage on a packet ship, as the owners of vessels found it more profitable to carry freight than passengers. Brothers Woodruff, Taylor, Clark, Mulliner, White and Turley had already gone to England, and Brother George A. Smith, on account of sickness, had gone to Philadelphia.

We were not idle, however, while we remained. We had calls to preach on every hand. I attended a meeting almost every night and was generally kept up talking till midnight or past.

As a result of our labors, many new members were added to the Church and fresh zeal was infused into the old ones. The Saints were very kind to us, and provided liberally for our wants, and when we were ready to sail they supplied us with money to pay our passage, and many tempting delicacies as well as more substantial food to serve us on the voyage, besides clothing and bedding.

In company with Elders Brigham Young, Orson Pratt, George A. Smith, Parley P. Pratt and R. Hedlock, I took passage for England on the ship *Patrick Henry*, on the 7th of March, 1840. A large number of the Saints came down to the wharf to bid us farewell. When we got into the small boat to go to the ship the Saints on shore sang "The Gallant Ship is Under Way," in which song we joined until the sound of our voices was lost in the distance. I may also add that previous to starting we held a conference with the Saints in New York, at which, by unanimous vote of those present, a "letter of recommendation" was given me, signed, in behalf of the Saints, by the presiding Elder of the Branch and clerk of the conference, testifying of my "wisdom, understanding, meekness and humility," and recommending me "as an upright, honest, candid man, and a faithful minister of the gospel."

CHAPTER XVII

INCIDENTS OF ELDER KIMBALL'S MISSION, AS GLEANED
FROM HIS LETTERS — SOME OF HIS PROPHECIES FULFILLED —
ELDER HYDE'S ACCOUNT OF THE CONTEST WITH EVIL SPIRITS —
GREAT SUCCESS OF THE WORK THROUGHOUT ENGLAND — A
TESTIMONIAL — SUMMARY OF LABORS — RETURN TO NAUVOO.

Elder Kimball's journal containing an account of his mission after leaving New York having been lost, it has been necessary to refer to letters written to his family for further particulars.

After a very stormy passage, he and his brethren arrived in Liverpool on the 6th of the April, 1840, where they met Elders Taylor and Fielding. Three days later he went by train to Preston. On reaching Penwortham, three miles from Preston he learned that the Saints had been anxiously expecting him for months. He found many friends standing by the railway watching for him. It was a happy meeting. There was great rejoicing among the Saints, and no little excitement and disgust among their enemies, who had declared that he and his associate Elders should never come to that land again. Many ministers were very much exercised over their presence and were in favor of petitioning the heads of government to interfere with their proselyting. They had cause to fear, as the labors of the Elders had already resulted in breaking up many churches.

On the 14th of April, the Elders met to organize, when Elder Willard Richards was ordained to the Apostleship and Brigham Young chosen President. The following day a general conference was held, at which one thousand seven hundred and twenty members of the Church were represented, exclusive of a large number scatted about in different parts of the land, whose standing was not known.

On the 18th, he accompanied Elder Willard Richards to the little branch at Walkerford, where, it will be remembered, Elder Kimball was first invited to come and preach by the Rev. Mr. Richards, whose daughter he had previously baptized. This daughter in the meantime had been married to Elder Willard Richards. And right here it may be as well to remark, in illustration of Elder Kimball's prophetic character, that this marriage was in fulfillment of a prediction which he made immediately after baptizing Miss Jeannette Richards. On meeting Elder Richards, he exclaimed, "Willard, I have baptized your wife to day!" A similar prediction was made by him about the marriage of Elder Joseph Fielding, and as literally fulfilled.

Since Elder Kimball's first visit to Walkerford, the few Saints there had suffered a great deal of persecution, still most of them had remained firm in the faith. It would appear, however, that Mr. John Richards had got to feel rather sore over the change in his prospects since having his church members converted to "Mormonism," for on seeing Elder Kimball again at his house in company with Elder Richards, he ordered him to leave. Brother Kimball, in writing of this, says: "I went out and pursued my journey. I could hear the old lady and Sister Richards crying when I got into the road. I felt to weep for them. She is a mother indeed, who has fed me and given me money and administered to my wants, and will not lose her reward."

Elder Kimball makes frequent mention of the love which the Saints manifested for him. While staying at the house of Brother Thomas Smith, in Clitheroe, he one morning overheard one of the daughters of the house say to her mother, "I want you should make Brother Kimball as comfortable as possible, and I will work in the factory as hard as I can."

His sympathy was frequently aroused by meeting with Saints who had been in comfortable circumstances when he knew them on his former mission, but who, through being thrown out of employment, were reduced to want, and would weep at not being able to set food before him as they had formerly done. In visiting Eccleston and Dauber's Lane and the surrounding region, he was received with a perfect ovation by the Saints, and they everywhere urged him to tarry with them. At a village called Chatburn, where he and Elder Fielding went to preach, no house could be found large enough for the people to convene in who turned out to hear them, and they held a meeting in a large barn, with most excellent results. Of this place and its people, he wrote: "Some who had left the Church wished they had been faithful; and some did return by humble repentance and being re-baptized. There appears to be something peculiar in the people of this place; others had tried in vain to enlist them in their folds, but on hearing the first preaching of the fullness of the gospel they were overwhelmed in tears of repentance and more than twenty were immediately baptized, which number was afterwards increased to about ninety, who have generally kept the faith. We have never received anything like an insult all the times we visited the village, and we feel bound to bless them."

On visiting Southport, a celebrated bathing place, and a great resort for rich people in search of health, he says, "There I beheld halt and blind, deaf and maimed and leprous. Such a distressed set of beings I never saw before. At this place there was a sister sick, and not expected to live. She was healed by administering the ordinances, and the next day she went with us two miles on foot."

Of the fraternal feeling that prevailed among the Saints, he says, "The rich love the poor so well they cannot bear to leave them behind. This is a celestial spirit; I would to God that all the Saints had it. There is one peculiarity about the people—just as soon as they come out of the water they want to go to America. When they begin to gather to Zion from this land, it will never stop till the salt is drained out of all nations. These are some of the jewels of the earth."

On the 4th of August he started on a visit to London, calling on the way at Burslem, where he remained and spent a holiday with the Saints and preached to six or seven thousand people in the public park. He also stopped at West Bromwich, Birmingham, Ledbury, Cheltenham, and several other places, and visited with the Saints, held a number of meetings and baptized quite a number. On reaching London, he went in search of the officers of the Teetotal Society, on account of the kindness they had shown him on his first mission, in opening their halls for him to preach in when others refused to. He found them very friendly and willing to assist him in any way possible. In company with Elders Woodruff and George A. Smith, he also visited Westminister Abbey and the Queen's Palace. In alluding to the latter and the lavish extravagance that he witnessed, he wrote, "Americans would be astonished to see the stir there is made over a little queen; at the same time there are thousands starving to death for want of a little bread; but they have their reward: 'Blessed are the poor, for they shall rejoice in the Holy One of Israel.' The rich have their reward here, and we shall have ours hereafter; so I do not envy them."

He found London the most difficult place to make any impression in of any that he had visited. It would seem as if the devil took special pains to do all he could to prevent the Elders from gaining a foothold there. On the 19th of September, while there, Elder Kimball was stricken with the cholera, and he felt as if he could not live till morning, but he rallied and commenced again as zealously as ever laboring for the conversion of the people. In writing of their discouraging labors, he said:

"Brother Woodruff had been gone about two weeks and we had baptized only one here in the city before he left. He felt almost discouraged, and said he never saw such a hard case before—every door closed against us, and every heart. We have traveled from day to day, from one part of the city to the other, to find some one that would receive our testimony. It seemed all in vain for some time; at last we found one old Cornelius that was ready to receive our testimony as soon as he heard it. On Sunday, the morning after I was taken with cholera, I went forward and baptized four. I thought it would do me good to go into a cold bath. Last night I went into the water and baptized four more. Some more are going on Sunday. The ice is broken in London, and the gospel has got such a hold that the devil can not root it out; but he is very mad, and I am glad—I shall never try to please him, the Lord assisting me. I see nothing to discourage me but everything to the reverse."

When the devil offers determined opposition, it may be considered as a sure indication that he is losing ground, and that his fears are awakened. Elder Kimball had had sufficient experience in contending with him to learn this fact, and to rejoice at seeing the evil one aroused. It will be remembered that the first success of the Elders in the English mission aroused hostility in that quarter, and Elders Kimball, Hyde and Russell had a personal contest with evil spirits. As the allusion to that occasion published on page 20 is quite brief [see chapter II, paragraph beginning with "One Saturday evening I was appointed by the brethren...."—Transcriber], it may be as well to insert here Elder Hyde's description of the scene, as contained in a letter to Elder Kimball, written May 22, 1856. He said:

"Every circumstance that occurred at that scene of devils is just as fresh in my recollection at this moment as it was at the moment of its occurrence, and will ever remain so. After you were overcome by them and had fallen, their awful rush upon me with knives, threats, imprecations and hellish grins amply convinced me that they were no friends of mine. While you were apparently senseless and lifeless on the floor and upon the bed (after we laid you there), I stood between you and the devils and fought them and contended against them face to face until they began to diminish in number, and to retreat from the room. The last imp that left turned round to me as he was going out and said, as if to apologize and appease my determined opposition to them, 'I never said anything against you!' I replied to him thus: 'It matters not to me whether you have or have not; you are a liar from the beginning! In the name of Jesus Christ, depart!' He immediately left, and the room was clear. That closed the scene of devils for that time."

In writing of London some time afterwards, Elder Kimball said, "The waters have begun to be troubled, and I pray that they may continue until the Lord gathers out His people from this city. I can say I never felt a greater desire for a place than I have for London, as it is the metropolis of the world and the depot of wickedness, for it don't seem as though any place could be any worse. All manner of debauchery that can be thought of is practiced here."

Elders Kimball and George A. Smith left London October 1, 1840, to attend the third general conference in Manchester, at which five of the Apostles met with the Saints and had a time of rejoicing. At this conference three thousand six hundred and twenty-six members were represented, more than double the number reported at the conference held six months before. From this showing the readers can judge of the rapidity with which the work had increased, and new fields were constantly opening up. The Elders met with powerful opposition in many places, but the more they were opposed the faster the work grew.

It would seem that among other things predicted upon the head of Elder Kimball by the Prophet previous to starting, was that he should see the queen of England. He records the fulfillment of this prediction as follows: "Elder Woodruff, Sister Ellen Redman, Dr. Copeland and wife, and I had a fair view of the queen. We saw her as the Prophet Joseph told us. * * * We stood within eight or nine feet of her when she passed and returned. She made her obeisance to us, and we returned it. She is a pleasant little body, but what a fuss there is made over one little girl; and how much more I would enjoy the privilege of sitting by my humble fireside with my wife and little children, and to see my brethren and sisters whom I have formed acquaintance with in days of affliction."

Though averse to royalty, as might be inferred from the foregoing, it would seem that he had a high regard personally for the Queen and her consort, Prince Albert, and he and his brethren presented each of them with a handsomely bound copy of the Book of Mormon, with their names upon them.

In February, 1841, in writing of the anxiety of the newly converted Saints to emigrate to America, he said, "I expect trouble is coming there as well as here. I feel as though I wanted to be there, and share with them, if they suffer. I would rather suffer affliction with the Saints of God than to have the pleasures of this world for a season; for to me it is all vanity. My prayer is that the Almighty will give me grace and patience to endure and hold on to the iron rod. If we do this, we shall do well. When He has spoken through His prophet or predicted anything on this Church, it has come to pass, and the honest have to suffer with the guilty. This has always been the case, but I pray the Lord to help me to fulfill, in all points of the law which leads to the celestial world."

He mentions a visit which he made to Bedford, where he remained a week and preached every night to crowded assemblies. He also baptized many, among whom were a number of the followers of a Mr. Matthews, a spurious Latter-day Saint preacher, who had baptized himself, and started out preaching faith, repentance, baptism, etc. He was a partner of Mr. Aitkin in Liverpool, and a man of considerable natural ability. Elder Kimball denounced him publicly, and when he took leave of Bedford, he "left the whole town in an uproar."

He also went to Birmingham, Manchester, Wales, Preston and Clitheroe, holding farewell meetings with the Saints, and baptizing more or less everywhere he went. At the latter place he was presented with the following

TESTIMONIAL:

"March 28, 1841.

"To all in these last days called to be Saints, and to the faithful in Christ Jesus, grace be to you, and peace from God, our Father, and from the Lord Jesus Christ.

"We, the brethren and sisters of the various churches associated in the conference assembling at Clitheroe, in the County of Lancaster, England, unitedly and with strong feelings of gratitude and affection, bear testimony that our brother, Elder Heber C. Kimball, has, in the midst of opposition and in the face of persecution and slander, diligently and faithfully labored as a servant of the Most High God; and we pray you in the name of Jesus Christ to receive him as such, rendering unto him every necessary assistance to aid him in the work of the Lord; and may the Spirit of Truth ever be with our brother, and with all the Saints of God. Amen.

"Signed on behalf of the conference,

"THOMAS WARD, Presiding Elder,

"STEPHEN LANGSTROFF."

On the 20th of April, 1841, he writes: "President Brigham Young, Orson Pratt, Wilford Woodruff, John Taylor, George A. Smith, Willard Richards and myself, with a company of one hundred and thirty Saints, are on board the ship *Rochester*, bound for New York. Brother P.P. Pratt and a multitude of the Saints came to bid us farewell, and many of them wept like children when we left them to return to our native land."

The following is from President Brigham Young's journal: "It truly seems a miracle to look upon the contrast between our landing and departure from Liverpool. We landed in the spring of 1840, as strangers in a strange land, and penniless, but through the mercy of God we have gained many friends, established churches in almost every noted town and city of Great Britain, baptized between 7,000 and 8,000 souls, printed 5,000 Books of Mormon, 3,000 hymn books, 2,500 volumes of the *Millennial Star* and 50,000 tracts; emigrated to Zion 1,000 souls, established a permanent shipping agency, which will be a great blessing to the Saints, and have left sown in the hearts of many thousands the seed of eternal life, which shall bring forth fruit to the honor and glory of God; and yet we have lacked nothing to eat, drink or wear; in all these things I acknowledge the hand of God."

Of his return home Elder Kimball records: "On the 1st of July, President Brigham Young, John Taylor and myself landed at Nauvoo, where we were met by the Prophet and a host of friends who had gathered there to welcome us home again."